You Shall Worship
One God

You Shall Worship One God

The Mystery of Loving Sacrifice in Salvation History

by Marie-Dominique Philippe, O.P.

Saint Benedict Press
Charlotte, North Carolina

Original title :
UN SEUL DIEU TU ADORERAS

Original translation by Dom Mark Pontifex
Revised by the Brothers and Sisters of Saint John

PERMISSU SUPERIORUM O.S.B

Nihil Obstat: Hubertus Richards, S.T.L., L.S.S.
            Censor Deputatus

Imprimatur: E. Morrogh Bernard
           Vicarius Generalis
           Westmonasterii: Die XXVII Maii MCMLIX

The Nihil Obstat *and* Imprimatur *are a declaration that a
book or pamphlet is considered to be free from doctrinal or moral error.
It is not implied that those who have granted the* Nihil Obstat *and*
Imprimatur *agree with the contents, opinions, or statements expressed.*

Cover design by Milo Persic. milo.persic@gmail.com

Cover image: The Ghent Altarpiece: main panel depicting The Adoration
of the Mystic Lamb, 1432 (oil on panel) (detail of 61235) by Hubert Eyck (c.
1370-1426) & Jan van (1390-1441) St. Bavo Cathedral, Ghent, Belgium/ ©
Paul Maeyaert/ The Bridgeman Art Library. Nationality / copyright
status: Flemish / out of copyright.

ISBN: 978-1935302-45-2

Printed and bound in the United States of America.

Saint Benedict Press
Charlotte, North Carolina
2010

CONTENTS

INTRODUCTION

O NLY insofar as man recognizes his Creator's sovereign rights over him can man fully be himself. If he does not discover God and does not recognize God's rights, but rather sees himself as his own master, he fails to discover the One who is his source and end. He is then like a traveler who has lost his way, knowing neither where he comes from nor where he is going.

That is why God attaches such importance, in His education of mankind, to the revelation of His mystery and to the first commandment, which enjoins worship. For it is by means of worship that man recognizes his absolute dependence upon God and enters into a personal relationship with his Creator and his Father. It is by means of adoration that man comes into God's presence and gains a practical knowledge of the goodness and sovereign majesty of his God.

Once man forgets the demands of the first commandment and allows himself to be carried away by sensible goods, by ambition for worldly glory and power, he diminishes himself and loses his true nobility. Instead of aiming at the knowledge and love of God, and thereby at gaining godlike ways, man turns back in on himself and seeks only to know and love himself. He supposes that man's true greatness consists, not in aiming at a God who is distant, "hypothetical," and even perhaps purely "imaginary," but in serving his fellow men, in loving and helping them and forgetting himself for their sakes. He supposes that true religion consists, not in adoring an unknown God, but in devoting himself to the well-being of his brethren and drawing them closer together. We must recognize that such a "substitution" (putting man in the place of God, turning the adoration of God into a means for social betterment) may be extremely attractive to one who has ceased to know what God is, or has never known, or at least has but a faint memory of it, and vaguely pictures God as an object of fear, a master always ready to punish. Such a "substitution" is surely nothing but a demonic secularization of what is most intimate to the Christian mystery.

At the Cross, Mary, the Woman, the Mother of mankind, took John in Jesus' place. Is she not to receive John as a mother to help him and dwell with him? As if this would cause her to give up her pure silent adoration! This ultimate union of love, which the Father brought about at the Cross between the Mother of His Son and John, was indeed a union achieved through the double observance of a single commandment: to love God and to love our neighbor— to love God in our brother, and our brother for God's sake, to recognize Jesus in His members and to love them with that same love which is reserved for Jesus. Thus, to the believer, there is no substitution brought about at the Cross since man is not put in God's place; but God raises man to

Himself and presents man as His own: "When you did it to one of the least of my brethren here, you did it to me" (cf. Mt. 25:40).

The act of adoration is not abolished to make way for mere service to mankind, but God makes use of worship that is silent, hidden, and spiritual to allow men to love one another more, to unite them in the bonds of a closer love, uniting mother to son and son to mother. That is the loving service which religion ordains and which should be practiced by the members of Christ in the new humanity purchased with Christ's blood. The jealous pride of the devil cannot endure such an exaltation of mankind. He seeks by every means to disfigure this new union of the Cross and to offer us a seductive caricature, which puts the Cross far away from us: God is dead. Men have slain God. They must now put themselves in God's place. They must shake off the tyrannical slavery of religion, which makes them acknowledge themselves as creatures of God. They must become aware of their own sovereignty, of their own absolute freedom. True religion should be philanthropic: man saves himself and saves his brethren. The Christian, however, instead of seeking for a new world and being seduced by this "new religion," this discovery of the new greatness of man, must understand with new clarity the act of adoration he performs so often yet so imperfectly. Faced with the false mysticism of the "superman" who is raised above all, the Christian must understand that more than ever he should, in the name of all humanity, worship his God, the Creator and Father of all life.

The Christian should be convinced that this is the most effective, indeed the only entirely effective, answer that he can give to his brethren who have rejected God and do not wish to hear about Him.

God Himself tells us this, and teaches it with the greatest emphasis in the Old Testament, when the people of Israel in Egypt, under the yoke of Pharaoh (the pharaohs are good representatives of the power of purely human efforts), allowed themselves to be seduced by prosperity, riches, material abundance, and earthly glory. They then forgot that they were called by God. God had called them and chosen them to be His people, to witness before all other nations that the Lord is the only God. God wished to snatch them from this tyranny; He could not suffer the misery and forgetfulness of His people. So He revealed Himself to Moses and told him what He willed: "I have seen the affliction of my people who are in Egypt, and have heard their cry because of their taskmasters; I know their sufferings, and I have come down to deliver them out of the hands of the Egyptians, and to bring them out of that land to a good and broad land, a land flowing with milk and honey" (Ex. 3:7-8).

It was by worship in the desert that the Lord wished to educate His people once again, to bring them back to Himself and to teach them their calling. Long contact with the riches and power of the Egyptians had turned Israel away from its God. In spite of this, the Lord watched over His people. And, in order to reawaken them to the truth, He wished to lead them into the desert and there, by means of adoration, set them face-to-face with their God in order to teach them to come into His presence.

Worship, then, is a voluntary act by which the creature freely and deliberately recognizes all the rights that God the

Creator has over it. Through worship, the creature recognizes that God is at the source of all that it is, that all that it is depends ultimately on God and is derived from Him, that the creature's whole life is subject to Him, and that He alone has the power of life and death since He is the author of life.

By means of adoration, the rational creature disappears before the face of God, recognizing that before the supreme majesty of the Creator he is nothing at all and knowing that he is not worthy to present himself alive before God: "mortal man cannot see me, and live to tell of it," Scripture says (cf. Ex. 33:20). This, then, is what worship brings about: it makes us die to ourselves in order to proclaim that God is first; the Lord God must be served first. That is why it is by and through worship alone that the rational creature truly presents himself before God, recognizing his incapacity to speak to Him and address Him, unless God raises him and draws him on.

Thus, worship plainly shows the gulf that exists between God and the creature. It is the act that teaches man in the most effective and emphatic way the mystery of God's transcendence and His sovereign majesty. Deep within his heart, the worshiper must discover not only his absolute and vital dependence on his Creator, but also his Creator's great mercy and real love; for, in adoration, this discovery is made by way of love. The purely speculative discovery a philosopher makes of his total dependence on God in the order of being, of the primacy of non-being in his own being, is always liable to cause him distress because this discovery is not pure and spiritual enough and the imagination may suddenly intervene. This distress then continues deep in his

mind, preventing him from thinking freely and contem-
plating Him who is the source of light. The distress easily
changes into an attitude of complete hostility and refusal.
Our poor human intellect cannot breathe the pure air of such
heights. This trouble—due both to metaphysics and to the
imagination—may often be at the root of some bitter forms
of atheism.[1]

On the other hand, in the free and voluntary act of adoration, God never appears as a rival or tyrant who crushes us
and holds us in slavery, but as a Father in the highest sense,
the Creator from whom comes all light, love, and life. In the
act of adoration, man recognizes the sovereign majesty of his
God and Creator, the loving presence of his almighty Father,
without seeing Him or knowing Him perfectly. Yet he is sure
that he is addressing a living being who sees into the depths
of his heart and is no stranger whom he does not know. Man's
act of adoration of God when God is not seen may be compared to the action of a child who, with his eyes still closed
and not yet having seen his mother's face, turns toward her
who can tend him, feed him, warm him, and protect him.
There is indeed a spiritual instinct that turns man's heart and
mind toward Him who alone can tend and protect him, but
this spiritual instinct needs to open out into a knowledge and
free choice, which becomes ever clearer.

---

1. We must never forget that, when dealing with realities above us and
beyond us, we can never know them as they really are unless we love
them. Only a loving knowledge allows us to become connatural with
them and understand them as they are. Otherwise, we are always liable
to underrate them, diminishing them to fit our own stature. Hence, we
can know God perfectly only through worship.

While the worship of God is not contemplation of God, nevertheless, there is no contradiction between them.[2] In the normal course, worship of God should open out into contemplation of God; it should be the approach to contemplation, to the intimate knowledge of God. The man who really worships God must seek to know Him more and more, as deeply as he possibly can. This knowledge will bring about an adoration that is more perfect, loving, and free. That is why worship plays an essential part in God's education of man, since it rouses in man a profound sense of the greatness of his God and Creator, of God's sovereign majesty, and of the depths of His being. The first commandment is not to know God, but to worship Him.

To obtain a better grasp of the importance and excellence of adoration, and of the way in which it should lead us to an intimate knowledge of God's mystery, we may first consider the great acts of worship that are described in the Old Testament. These great acts take place in sacrifices, since sacrifice as such is nothing else than the worship of the whole man, body and soul, king of the universe, recognizing officially the sovereign rights of God over him, over his goods, all his conduct, and all his relationships.

---

2. Worship, which is based on the virtue of religion, is in some sense a matter of justice. Contemplation, which is based on wisdom, the gift of wisdom, is a matter of charity, friendship with God. It would be very interesting to analyze the precise connection between justice and friendship in human life, in order to show by analogy the relation between worship and contemplation. There can be no friendship without justice, no true contemplation without worship. Friendship is the final end of justice, contemplation, of worship.

The acts of worship in the great Old Testament sacrifices are privileged meeting places between man and God. Each of the different sacrifices expresses a particular aspect of adoration and prefigures the great sacrifice of Christ on the Cross. It is indeed Christ on the Cross who alone reveals to us the mystery of worship in its entirety and at the same time reveals, in an ultimate way, the whole mystery of God as Love.

We shall see, then, in the first chapter of this book, the worship offered in the great Old Testament sacrifices, which prefigures the worship of the unique sacrifice; in the second, we shall try to examine thoroughly the loving adoration of this unique sacrifice; finally, in the third chapter, in the light of Christ crucified, we shall try to see how this worship gives us a better understanding of God's mystery, of its characteristics and divine perfection. The act of adoration upon the Cross is the royal way to the contemplation of God's mystery.

You Shall Worship
One God

CHAPTER 1

THE OLD TESTAMENT SACRIFICES: TYPES OF THE SACRIFICE OF THE CROSS

SACRIFICES BEFORE THE LAW

The Sacrifice of Abel

THE first action of the children of Adam and Eve that Scripture reveals to us is one of offering: "Cain brought to the Lord an offering of the fruit of the ground, and Abel brought of the firstlings of his flock and of their fat portions" (Gen. 4:3-4). That is a most natural action for man to perform: he offers to the Lord the fruit of his labor, thereby recognizing that God is the sovereign master of the fertility of the earth and of animals.

In the case of Abel, this simple action was the expression of a deep conviction, coloring his whole life. For him, this offering was the recognition of God's absolute right over his goods and over himself, and his sole intention was to proclaim the glory of his God, the one important thing in his eyes. Hence, in making this offering, he looked only to God, without thinking of his brother or his brother's conduct, and

1

without troubling himself about the way in which he approached God. Abel was a man of absolute sincerity. When he offered the firstborn of his flock to God, this outward action corresponded to the inner intention of his soul, for he recognized the sovereign rights of God over the fertility of life. In sacrificing to God the firstborn of his flock, his soul offered itself to God; it hid itself in the majesty of its God and desired only to concern itself with God's sovereign greatness. Scripture tells us this in a veiled form, with the greatest simplicity, but plainly enough, when we compare the Lord's attitude toward Abel with His attitude toward Cain: "And the Lord had regard for Abel and his offering, but for Cain and his offering He had no regard" (Gen. 4:4). In the anthropomorphic language of Scripture, it is easy to see that Abel looked to the Lord beyond the offering he made to God; the offering was a means of coming into the presence of God. Cain, on the other hand, performed only the external action of offering. He did not look to the Lord, but, being jealous of his brother, he spied on him. His heart was turned away from God and turned wholly toward his brother, not out of brotherly care, but out of envy and jealousy. He could not endure that his younger brother should be so attentive to God and so attracted by Him, and this annoyed and grieved him.

In spite of the rebuke addressed to him by the Lord, in spite of his conscience, which told him that such grief was wrong (it was not right for him to grieve at his brother's happiness, at the care with which God treated younger sons, to be angry with his brother because he had done his duty as he saw it in all sincerity), Cain let himself be carried away with anger and jealousy. The presence of his brother became increasingly unendurable. The only possible means of satisfying his jealousy was to get rid of him, to murder him.

It was jealousy against a brother in a matter of religion that provoked the first murder, the first fratricide. Cain's jealousy, which led to murder, shows us clearly the absoluteness of Abel's offering: it affected his whole life. By declaring that God was the master of the fertility of his flocks, he recognized that God had the fullest rights over his life and that he belonged to God. Hence, he put everything in God's hands and surrendered himself to Him with such simplicity. Such an act of worship has an absolute character, for it binds man to Him who is his Creator and at the same time separates him from all that is not his God.

By attacking Abel, who worshiped his God, Cain made a direct attack on God, for he who worships God is wrapped in God's sovereign majesty. God is his refuge. Cain, having failed to recognize in his heart God's absolute rights over him by true worship, was unable to listen to God when He wished to correct him, although he was to be forced to recognize God's rights and submit to them. The anger of the Lord fell upon him. Cain, having failed to recognize with all sincerity that the fruitfulness of the earth comes from God, had to recognize the curse of the earth: "Till that ground, and it will yield thee its fruit no longer; thou shalt be a wanderer, a fugitive on earth." Undergoing this punishment, he learned to recognize the absolute authority of God, who is the Creator. This first offering of adoration proclaimed God as master of the fruitfulness of the earth and of living things.

In contradiction to this first act, which sprung from the heart of man and rose toward God, we are shown the devil's first caricature of worship. Outwardly all was perfect, but the intention in the heart did not correspond with the outward action of offering. Outwardly there was a gift, an offering, but inwardly there was fierce jealousy and desire to rule: we cannot worship God if we do not love our brother, as our Lord emphatically declares (Mt. 5:23-24).

Noah's Sacrifice After the Flood

> The Lord saw that the wickedness of man was great in the earth, and that every imagination of the thoughts of his heart was only evil continually. And the Lord was sorry that he had made man on the earth, and it grieved him to his heart. So the Lord said, "I will blot out man whom I have created from the face of the ground". . . . But Noah found favor in the eyes of the Lord (Gen. 6:5-8).

We know how, by means of the flood, God carried out His plan "to blot out mankind from the face of the earth," and how He protected Noah by commanding him to build an ark. After the flood, God ordered Noah to come out of the ark, and Noah's first act was to build an altar to the Lord:

> Then Noah built an altar to the Lord, and took of every clean animal and of every clean bird, and offered burnt offerings on the altar. And when the Lord smelled the pleasing odor, the Lord said in his heart, "I will never again curse the ground because of man, for the imagination of man's heart is evil from his

youth; neither will I ever again destroy every
living creature as I have done. While the earth
remains, seedtime and harvest, cold and heat,
summer and winter, day and night, shall not
cease" (Gen. 8:20-22).

This sacrifice of thanksgiving, made immediately after
the flood, although already more well thought out and more
religious than the first two (with the construction of the altar
and the distinction of clean animals), still appears as a very
spontaneous act of man and the head of human society. It
was the first answer that Noah gave to his God and Savior
when God returned to him the land after having cleansed it.
Having escaped the danger of death, man thanked God for
His providential assistance, His brotherly help, while also
acknowledging the justice of His anger and punishment.
Noah's sacrifice was no longer the simple act of offering, of
worship, of the creature who recognizes the sovereign rights
of the Creator; it was an act of thanksgiving and reparation,
acknowledging that God's action was to be praised, that it
was full of wisdom, justice, and mercy.

The sacrifice of Noah, the new head of the human society,
was all-embracing. It was the whole living world, the whole
world cleansed by God, that was offered to God and accepted
by Him. We see this clearly from the answer God gave:
"And when the Lord smelled the pleasing odor, the Lord said
in His heart, 'I will never again curse the ground because of
man.'"

Gratitude always touches God's heart profoundly, and
God replied to the sacrifice of thanksgiving by a covenant

that embraced the whole physical world: "While the earth remains, seed-time and harvest, cold and heat . . . shall not cease." It was a covenant of fertility and peace: God blessed Noah and his children and said to them:

> Be fruitful and multiply, and fill the earth. The fear of you and the dread of you shall be upon every beast of the earth, and upon every bird of the air, upon everything that creeps on the ground and all the fish of the sea; into your hand they are delivered. Every moving thing that lives shall be food for you; and as I gave you the green plants, I give you everything. Only you shall not eat flesh with its life, that is, its blood. For your lifeblood I will surely require a reckoning; of every beast I will require it and of man; of every man's brother I will require the life of man. Whoever sheds the blood of man, by man shall his blood be shed; for God made man in his own image (Gen. 9:1-6).
>
> Behold, I establish my covenant with you . . . Never again shall all flesh be cut off by the waters of a flood . . . And God said, "This is the sign of the covenant which I make between me and you and every living creature that is with you, for all future generations: I set my bow in the cloud" (Gen. 9:9-13).

By giving to man such universal power over all living beings, God reminded him of the nobility of his nature: he is an image of God. Promising man that he would never repeat the flood, God gave man a sign of peace so that he might not forget the peaceful covenant that God had made with mankind and with the world. This covenant demanded a greater faithfulness from man, for God put more trust in him, leaving him a greater responsibility.

By this sacrifice of thanksgiving, by this adoration of gratitude, God joined man more fully with Himself in His dominion, leaving to man's care the government of the world, while reminding him that "man's heart is evil from his youth" (Gen. 8:21).

The Sacrifice of Isaac

The sacrifices of Abel and of Noah were real archetypes, having in some sense a universal application. Their actions expressed a religious attitude, the attitude of a man who is naturally and supernaturally directed toward God and who puts all his trust in God. Abel, cast aside by his brother, found his refuge in God. Noah, worshiping God and thanking Him for His protection, was called by God to live in peace, to make a covenant with Him.

With Abraham, however, the history of the people of Israel begins. Everything starts with the gratuitous summons by God, an imperative call: "Go from your country"; and a summons so full of trust and promise: "I will make of you a great nation" (Gen. 12:1-2). This was a wonderful annunciation on God's part, and Abraham silently gives his "fiat," carrying out God's command.

Having chosen Abraham, God gradually revealed Himself to him, showing Himself to him, blessing him, and making

a covenant with him. And Abraham replied by building altars
to God, recognizing Him as God, as having full rights over him.

With the perspective we have chosen, one fact stands
out in all the personal relationships uniting the Lord with the
one whom He had chosen. After the birth of Isaac, which
Abraham had looked forward to with such hope and which
came about in so wonderful a way, when Abraham was filled
with joy and pride, God then wished to try him. "After these
things God tested Abraham," we are told by Scripture. "He
said to him, 'Abraham!' And he said, 'Here am I.' He said,
'Take your son, your only son Isaac, whom you love, and go
to the land of Moriah, and offer him there as a burnt offering upon one of the mountains of which I shall tell you.' So
Abraham rose early in the morning" (Gen. 22:1-3).

This time it is God who takes the first step, who demands this sacrifice to test the fidelity of His servant and
friend. It is God who decides the matter for the holocaust and
when it shall be carried out. After having filled Abraham with
favors and having given him this child and promised him so
much, God demands an offering of all he possesses. God
insists, with apparent cruelty, "Take your only son, your
beloved son Isaac." God asks this father to sacrifice his
beloved son as a holocaust, to show his love, beyond all else,
for God the Lord. God asks Abraham to destroy for His sake
what He has freely given him, the gift that was the special
sign of His love. He demands it in order to probe Abraham's
heart, to see how far his faithfulness reaches.

To human reason, there appears to be a kind of contradiction in God's conduct, for it is not merely a question of His giving and taking back, but of giving after having intensified the

desire by promising, partially fulfilling, promising again, and finally fulfilling by an almost miraculous gift. It is indeed a question of giving with all the generosity of a sovereign God, then of demanding from those who were favored by the gift its total destruction, that they might declare by this destruction the sovereign rights of the giver.

However terrible might be the demands of God, Abraham, as a faithful servant, obeyed at once; he rose up quickly. He set out to fulfill God's order completely. Such was his faith that he did not hesitate for an instant to accept God's word. Without discussion, he submitted to the conditions of the sacrifice. He submitted to the worship of God in the way desired by God Himself, acknowledged His sovereign, absolute rights. Scripture describes this with remarkable restraint:

> He cut the wood for the burnt offering, and arose and went to the place of which God had told him. On the third day Abraham lifted up his eyes and saw the place afar off. Then Abraham said to his young men, "Stay here with the ass; I and the lad will go yonder and worship, and come again to you." And Abraham took the wood of the burnt offering, and laid it on Isaac his son; and he took in his hand the fire and the knife. So they went both of them together. And Isaac said to his father Abraham, "My father!" And he said, "Here am I, my son." He said, "Behold, the fire and the wood; but where is the lamb for a burnt

offering?" Abraham said, "God will provide himself the lamb for a burnt offering, my son." So they went both of them together (Gen. 22:3-8).

We should notice the father's silence as he climbed the mountain of sacrifice. In the presence of his son, Abraham could only keep silent, a silence hard to bear, and harder still as he came nearer to the place and the time when he was to slay his own son. With the greatest care, Abraham jealously kept secret the order received from God, which struck him to the heart yet also gave him the power to go forward. By keeping this divine secret in faith, he becomes divinely estranged from his son, whom he must sacrifice in a few minutes. He could only do this provided that he became a mere instrument of God in the fullest degree, that God's command first immolated his father's heart, transforming him into a "blind servant," blind to all that did not concern the divine order, blind to his own feelings as a father and the terrible consequences of his act. The sole thought of the consequences of the act, which he was freely performing and living minute after minute, would have repulsed his father's heart and prevented him from taking another step. All his energy had to be absorbed by this command of God, if he was to accept it without discussion and with heroic faith.

Isaac, the child of laughter and of promise, well beloved, was walking freely and joyfully beside his father, all the time calling him Father, as if nothing was happening, in utter ignorance. With a child's curiosity, he questioned his father and at once put the dreadful question, the only question possible:

"Father, where is the lamb we need for a victim?" That was the great question, throughout the Old Testament, to which John the Baptist would give the answer.

The instrument carrying out God's order, faithfully and promptly, knew only too well where the lamb was. But the father, whose torn heart was suddenly awakened by this tender appeal from his son calling him father, could say nothing; for he knew nothing else and could understand nothing else than utter abandonment to God's mercy: "My son, God will see to it that there is a lamb to be sacrificed." He had not chosen the lamb for the sacrifice, but God Himself had.

> When they came to the place of which God had told him, Abraham built an altar there, and laid the wood in order, and bound Isaac his son, and laid him on the altar, upon the wood. Then Abraham put forth his hand and took the knife to slay his son. But the angel of the Lord called to him from heaven, and said, "Abraham, Abraham!" And he said, "Here am I." He said, "Do not lay your hand on the lad or do anything to him; for now I know that you fear God, seeing you have not withheld your son, your only son, from me" (Gen. 22:9-12).

All was ready, everything prepared. Only at the very moment when Abraham began the movement to sacrifice his son, the angel of the Lord intervenes and calls to him, "Do not lay your hand on the lad." The ram outwardly took the place of the child and was offered as a holocaust.

This sacrifice shows clearly that the outward slaying of the ram was of quite secondary importance. This was not what God valued most highly but rather the intention with which it was done, the inner sacrifice, the worship of the heart. This was essentially the sacrifice of Abraham and not of Isaac. It was an inner testing, a testing of Abraham's fidelity, of the quality of his love for God. God carried this testing to its extreme limit in order that the truly heroic quality of the servant's fidelity might be shown more plainly, the fidelity of the friend of God, despite all of the apparent contradictions in God's conduct toward him.

It is easy to grasp the entirely new character of this sacrifice, which no longer appealed only to the acquired or infused virtue of religion—like the first two types of offering, those of Abel and Noah—but demanded at once and explicitly the virtue of obedience, exercised in the light of a living and loving faith. The virtue of religion, taken in itself, consists in giving to God what is due to Him. That is why it falls under the category of justice, as a form of justice: it is justice toward God. Among the acquired moral virtues, it is in one sense pre-eminent because it is the virtue that draws us nearest to God. It is concerned immediately with His service, His worship, and His praise. For this reason, it develops in a special way in man that which makes him God's image, that which binds him to God, that which makes him capable of entering into a relationship with God. It is indeed the characteristic human virtue, insofar as man is a rational creature, entirely subject to the Creator and King of the universe. Upon our deep-seated, natural desire for God, it throws a certain light, derived from human reason, making this desire more consciously dependent, more thoroughly directed toward God in His unique mystery.

The virtue of religion is like an eminent virtue of politeness, which teaches us to live as creatures ought to live in relation to God, to conduct ourselves properly in His hidden presence and in the presence of all that belongs to Him. But this politeness is intimate and interior; it is a politeness of the soul, although it is expressed by certain actions. It is a politeness that is expressed by complete devotion to God and self-effacement in God's presence.

Together with grace and charity, we are given the infused virtue of religion, which we exercise in the light of faith and address in the first place to the loving majesty of the Father. The exercise of this infused virtue of religion can receive a final development from the gift of piety. Breathed on by the gift of piety, adoration becomes in the full sense a filial adoration, the adoration of the well-beloved son.

Abraham obeyed God's command; and it was specifically through this act of obedience that he recognized the sovereign rights of God over him and that he adored the will which his human intelligence could not fathom. Sacrifice, then, consists in the first place in the act of obedience to God's word. Abraham's act of obedience concerned the very person whom he loved most upon earth. It was not the firstborn of his flock, nor the clean animals, that Abraham was commanded to slay in order to declare the omnipotence of the Creator, but that very thing which made him a patriarch and which he loved more than himself—all his hope and joy, his only son.

By this act of obedience, God plainly wished to remind Abraham that the Creator has the right of life and death over all that exists, all that lives. He can require a father to sacrifice to Him his son; and the father cannot, as a mere creature before God, claim the rights he holds from God; he can only be silent and obey. But God never acts in this way simply by His sovereign authority, for that would be tyrannical, and God would no longer be acting as God and Father of His creatures.

God requires this act of obedience from Abraham to test the fidelity of His servant and friend, still more of His friend than of His servant. (The fidelity of the servant need not go so far as this, for the servant is faithful if he fulfills perfectly the task demanded of him.) The friend is faithful if his heart is in closer and closer harmony with the heart of his friend, if his love for his friend is more and more a love deliberately chosen. If God wishes to test the fidelity of his friend, it is in order to reveal His own fidelity as a friend. The fidelity of God is such that, even though the external circumstances seem to contradict it, the contradictions are only in appearance; and behind these appearances, His love is unalterable. It was in fact God who gave to Abraham his son Isaac; and if He caused Abraham to suffer this test, it was in order to give him Isaac all the more completely.

That is why the act of obedience, required for the sacrifice, appealed directly to the patriarch's faith, hope, and love of God. Such an act of obedience can be practiced only in virtue of a pure, unreasoning faith that does not doubt God's word but is prepared to accept its divine meaning and to disregard the apparent contradictions and absurdities. Abraham, father of believers, must believe in God's faithfulness and God's promise without wishing to justify it in his own eyes.

If Abraham had not immediately submitted his obedience to the light of faith, if he had judged it by his own experience, his acquired prudence, he would have fallen into terrible distress, which would have almost paralyzed him.

To carry out God's order, he had to be willing to act under God's inspiration, without understanding. The prudence he possessed as a patriarch had to give up its most lawful and fully human rights in the face of God's demands, which only faith could grasp. In order to become the patriarch of God's people, Abraham had to give up the use of his own experience in this great and so important matter and had to rely only on the wisdom of God. In order to enter into God's ways, and to act in accordance with them, he had to abandon all, offer all, and sacrifice all.

By this act of obedience, the patriarch was asked to destroy his only grounds for hope, both human and divine: the son who was the first fulfillment of God's promise and his only heir. His hope in this act of obedience had to go beyond that grounds which was so lawful, to lose all support and rely only on the merciful omnipotence of the Father. In carrying out God's command during those three days when he climbed up to the mountain, Abraham had to hope in God against all human hope: "Go from your country and your kindred and your father's house to the land that I will show you" (Gen. 12:1).

We have to leave all that is natural to us in order to obey this imperative order and command of God: "Come." Abraham, having listened to God with joy, listened to Him with sorrow, for he not only had to leave his son but had to offer him in sacrifice. There could no longer be a promised land

for Abraham, since the sacrifice involved the destruction of
him who was the true promised land. He had then to hope
only in the almighty mercy of God.

We have already seen that, in God's plan, the point of
this trial was to purify the fidelity in the heart of His friend.
In this act of obedience, God asked Abraham to love Him
more than His gifts, love Him above the wonderful gift he
had received in Isaac. The act of obedience expressed the
choice of love, which God alone could demand. To choose
God by sacrificing Isaac, sacrificing what the human heart of
Abraham loved most, was truly to put God before everything
and everybody. It was to witness that God alone is love, that
God alone suffices.

In essentials, this sacrifice was an act of adoration, the
fruit of the theological virtues of faith, hope, and charity.
Hence, it came from the depths of his being. This sacrifice
occurs first and foremost in the heart of the patriarch Abraham. In the depths of his soul, he distinguished in a new way
between the divine and human. God required of him an exercise of faith so exacting that human prudence and reason
were silenced; God required so sheer an act of hope that every
human motive and support were left aside; God required so
pure an act of love that all human love, however lawful, was
as nothing.

Although the sacrifice demanded was not carried out
externally and at the last moment was completely altered,
inwardly it was fully accomplished. Abraham had lived those
three days with an extraordinary intensity, the presence of
Isaac adding to it still more. To the inward sacrifice of faith,
hope, and love, there corresponds a new covenant between

God and Abraham. With a fresh generosity of love for His servant and friend, who had been so faithful and so generous and who was willing to offer to Him in holocaust the only offspring of his race, God responds with the promise of a wonderful fruitfulness, descendants without number: "By myself I have sworn, says the Lord, because you have done this, and have not withheld your son, your only son, I will indeed bless you, and I will multiply your descendants as the stars of heaven and as the sand which is on the seashore. And your descendants shall possess the gate of their enemies, and by your descendants shall all the nations of the earth bless themselves, because you have obeyed my voice" (Gen. 22:16-18).

Indeed God had already promised to Abraham a great posterity: "I will make your descendants as the dust of the earth; so that if one can count the dust of the earth, your descendants also can be counted"(Gen. 13:16). " 'Look toward heaven, and number the stars, if you are able to number them.' Then he said to him, 'So shall your descendants be' " (Gen. 15:5).

God had already made a covenant with him: "Behold, my covenant is with you, and you shall be the father of a multitude of nations" (Gen. 17:4). "I will establish my covenant with [Isaac] as an everlasting covenant for his descendants after him" (Gen. 17:19). After the heroic act of obedience, God pledges himself: "By myself I have sworn . . ." and God gives him an abundant blessing, which then becomes universal (catholic): "by your descendants shall all the nations of the earth bless themselves, because you have obeyed my voice" (Gen. 22:16, 18).

This inward sacrifice, carried out through obedience, introduces us to a deeper contemplation of God's mystery. It is no longer only the omnipotence of the Creator and Father which is experienced through this act of adoration, but truly the fidelity of His love. God reveals Himself as the Friend, in the strictest sense.

SACRIFICES UNDER THE LAW

The Passover

The story of Isaac, Jacob, and Joseph shows us in a remarkable way how God guides His friends, those whom He has chosen and with whom He has made a covenant; but, from the perspective we have taken in this study, their story adds nothing to the great sacrifice we have just considered, for this dominates the whole of Genesis.[3] The Lord had said to Abraham, "Know of a surety that your descendants will be sojourners in a land that is not theirs, and will be slaves there, and they will be oppressed for four hundred years" (Gen. 15:13).[4]

---

3. If we wish to consider in detail the meetings of God with man, Jacob's dream (Gen. 28:10-19) must be specially mentioned, since it is the revelation of a special presence of God—just as the struggle of Jacob with the unknown being who did not give his name (Gen. 32:23-33) is the revelation of God in a kind of struggle between friends. Here it is not a question of acts of adoration or of sacrifice but rather of contemplation. The story of Joseph shows us the friendly cooperation of God with the man He has chosen to save His people from famine after being rejected by his own family, hidden in the cistern and sold to the Egyptians (Gen. 34:12-31).

4. Cf. Ex. 12:40: "The time that the people of Israel dwelt in Egypt was four hundred and thirty years."

It was Moses whom the Lord chose to deliver His people from the yoke of the Egyptians. From Moses' birth, we find that God treated him with a special care (Ex. 2:1-10). It was on the mountain of God, Horeb, that "the angel of the Lord appeared to him in a flame of fire out of the midst of a bush" (Ex. 3:2). God called to him: " 'Moses, Moses!' And he said, 'Here am I.' Then he said, 'Do not come near; put off your shoes from your feet, for the place on which you are standing is holy ground. . . . I am the God of your father, the God of Abraham, the God of Isaac, and the God of Jacob.' And Moses hid his face, for he was afraid to look at God" (Ex. 3:4-6).

There will be no attempt here to analyze the wonderful meeting between God and Moses—when God revealed to Moses the loving and merciful care that He had for His people; when God finally gave him the order to go to Pharaoh as His emissary to lead His people out of Egypt; and when Moses, faced with this unexpected order, hung back and tried to make excuses for himself, trying to escape from a mission that terrified him. Had he not withdrawn to the land of Midian to escape from Pharaoh, who wished to destroy him? Now he must present himself before Pharaoh. Moses thought more of himself and his own safety than of that of his people.

When Moses, having agreed, asked Him who had declared Himself the God of his fathers what His message was—in order that he might be able to present himself to Pharaoh with greater authority—God, in answer to this demand, said of Himself: "I AM WHO AM." It is, however, absolutely necessary for us to understand well that this personal revelation of God to Moses directly commanded the sacrifice of the Passover.

So Moses was sent by the Lord with this precise mission: to get permission from Pharaoh for the people of Israel to "go a three days' journey into the wilderness, that we may sacrifice to the Lord our God" (Ex. 3:18). Since Pharaoh would not agree to obey the Lord willingly, God forced him with a strong hand by signs and portents, in order to frighten Pharaoh—showing him that his power was nothing compared with the power of the Lord. The last of these portents had a special character: it had both to prepare the people of Israel religiously and also punish all the families of the Egyptians. For Israel, it was the sacrifice of the Passover; for the Egyptians, it was the death of their firstborn. It was the passing over of God, who protected and saved His own people and punished the pride and tyranny of Pharaoh.

In order to understand the true nature of the sacrifice of the Passover, which was to play such an important part in the religious life of the people of Israel and which was to be completed on the Cross, we must always return to Exodus 12.

> The Lord said to Moses and Aaron in the land of Egypt, "This month shall be for you the beginning of months; it shall be the first month of the year for you. Tell all the congregation of Israel that on the tenth day of this month they shall take every man a lamb according to their fathers' houses, a lamb for a household; and if the household is too small for a lamb, then a man and his neighbor next

to his house shall take according to the number of persons; according to what each can eat you shall make your count for the lamb. Your lamb shall be without blemish, a male a year old; you shall take it from the sheep or from the goats; and you shall keep it until the fourteenth day of this month, when the whole assembly of the congregation of Israel shall kill their lambs in the evening. Then they shall take some of the blood, and put it on the two doorposts and the lintel of the houses in which they eat them. They shall eat the flesh that night, roasted; with unleavened bread and bitter herbs they shall eat it. Do not eat any of it raw or boiled with water, but roasted, its head with its legs and its inner parts. And you shall let none of it remain until the morning, anything that remains until the morning you shall burn. In this manner you shall eat it: your loins girded, your sandals on your feet, and your staff in your hand; and you shall eat it in haste. It is the Lord's passover. For I will pass through the land of Egypt that night, and I will smite all the firstborn in the land of Egypt, both man and beast; and on all the gods of Egypt I will execute judgments: I am the Lord. The blood shall be a sign for you, upon the houses where you are; and when I see the blood, I will pass over you, and no plague shall fall upon you to destroy you,

when I smite the land of Egypt. This day shall
be for you a memorial day, and you shall keep
it as a feast to the Lord; throughout your generations you shall observe it as an ordinance
for ever" (Ex. 12:1-14).

Upon Moses' orders, all that the Lord commanded was
carried out. This family meal was a religious meal; then was
eaten "the sacrifice of the Lord's passover, for he passed over
the houses of the people of Israel in Egypt, when he slew the
Egyptians but spared our houses" (Ex. 12:27), as Moses
declared to the elders.[5]

"It was a night," Scripture tells us, speaking of the carrying out of what had been proclaimed, "of watching by the
Lord, to bring them out of the land of Egypt; so this same
night is a night of watching kept to the Lord by all the people of Israel throughout their generations" (Ex. 12:42).[6]

Without pausing over all the details of the Passover, we
may simply notice that we are in the presence of an entirely new
sacrifice, which is presented to us as determined by the Lord.

---

5. *Victima transitus domini est,* says the Vulgate. Moses adds when addressing
   the people and recalling the miraculous assistance of the Lord: "And it
   shall be to you as a sign on your head and as a memorial between your
   eyes, that the law of the Lord may be in your mouth; for with a strong
   hand the Lord has brought you out of Egypt" (Ex. 13:9). Cf. Num.
   9:1-14, where the Passover is presented as the offering to the Lord.

6. Cf. Ex. 12:43-46, when the Lord gives Moses and Aaron further
   instruction as to the celebration of the Passover: "No foreigner shall
   eat of it. . . . In one house shall it be eaten; you shall not carry forth any
   of the flesh outside the house; and you shall not break a bone of it."

By this new institution, God wishes to take His people in hand, to give them a fresh sense of their religious calling. He wished, while granting them their freedom, to renew the will of their youth, as was plainly signified by the season when the Passover was to be celebrated: "This month shall be for you the beginning of months; it shall be the first month of the year for you" (Ex. 12:2; 12:41; Num. 9:1). This sacrifice, this offering, was carried out at a religious meal, a family meal among believers only, during the night and in haste.

The Passover implies a victim: "Your lamb shall be without blemish, a male a year old; you shall take it from the sheep or from the goats" (Ex. 12:5; Lev. 22:19 ff.). Later, the custom prevailed of sacrificing a lamb that was slain, whose blood was a sign of protection when sprinkled "on the two doorposts and the lintel of the houses." The sacrifice of this victim was performed in honor of the Lord, to proclaim that He is the only true God, the God of Israel, and also to save the family of Israel from the immolation of the firstborn.

Thus, the Passover shows the different judgments pronounced by the Lord on Egypt and Israel: to Egypt, the passing by of God brought destruction, death, and terror; to Israel, it brought freedom and safety. The Passover implies public worship, for by the celebration of this rite, the Lord is recognized as the God who has saved His people, who alone can deliver His people from the yoke of Pharaoh.

This act of adoration looks both to God's saving mercy and to His avenging justice. It is under the influence of charity and of the gift of piety that adoration can attain the saving mercy of God the Father, who, full of pity for His children and wishing for them to suffer no longer under the rule of a foreigner, takes them directly under His protection. Such an act of adoration is performed with a certain divine familiarity, which yet reverences the sovereign majesty of Him who said, "I am the God who is," and who exercised His sovereign right of life and death over the whole people of Egypt when they were oppressing those whom He loved. Hence, it is quite natural that such an act of adoration should be offered during a family meal, when all the members are sharing in the fatherly mercy shown that night, in great intimacy, while still maintaining a great solemnity.

For this reason, too, although the Law had so many different liturgies for different sacrifices, yet the Passover always remained the supreme sacrifice of the people of Israel—that religious people consecrated to God. For this reason again, when the Temple, the house of God, was built, the principal sacrifice of the Mosaic Law was not offered within the precincts of the Temple or reserved to the Levites like other sacrifices, but continued to be offered at home by the father of the family. Hence it was that this sacrifice seemed to escape the legalism of the Law, which to a great extent pervaded the whole liturgy of the Temple. This sacrifice remained, as it were, the most spiritual element in the people of Israel, its religious soul. We can understand why God began to re-educate His people by means of this sacrifice. As we have said, this sacrifice declared God's almighty mercy and involved the loving worship of a Son who abandoned Himself to the Father's mercy. To take responsibility for someone, to re-educate him and teach him afresh, his complete confidence must be gained. But consider the difficulty of reviving confidence in a heart that has grown cold, generation after generation for four centuries! That is why God, in His wisdom, made use of a means profoundly and essentially human: a family meal. He showed openly that all His power would be used in mercy to His people, that they might understand that this family meal could, by God's will, become a religious meal, a sacrifice that declared the mercy of God's majesty and allowed them to share in His saving mercy. Through this act of filial worship, this close communion with the mercy of the Lord, Israel gained confidence again in its God and again found freedom.[7]

From that time on, Israel was to be able to serve its God in the desert and to become a religious people, a people who belonged to the Lord alone, reserved for Him. It is from this unique perspective that we must understand the tablets of the Law, the commandments of God given on Mount Sinai (Ex. 31:18).

The laws were religious and fatherly:

> And God spoke all these words, saying, "I am the Lord your God, who brought you out of the land of Egypt, out of the house of bondage. You shall have no other gods before me. You shall not make for yourself a graven image, or any likeness of anything that is in

---

7. The Passover was connected to the Sabbath, expressing an idea of liberation: every Sabbath, and especially the Passover, should free the people of God from servile work. The Sabbatical year was also a year of rest and freedom. During this year, special trust had to be placed in God, for this period of rest was for God's glory (Lev. 25:10).

heaven above, or that is in the earth beneath, or that is in the water under the earth; you shall not bow down to them or serve them; for I the Lord your God am a jealous God, visiting the iniquity of the fathers upon the children to the third and the fourth genera- tion of those who hate me, but showing stead- fast love to thousands of those who love me and keep my commandments. . . . Remember the sabbath day, to keep it holy" (Ex. 20:1-8).

These commandments were intended to educate a reli- gious people who recognized that there is but one true God, worthy to be worshiped, a jealous God, who loved His peo- ple "jealously." The Law showed the "jealousy" of God for His people. This divine jealousy obviously had not the same meaning as jealousy for us, which results from an overly self- ish love. God's jealousy expressed His overwhelming love for His people and the intensity of His mercy. He is a God who loves, and in this He differs from idols and false gods.

The sacrifice of the Passover, therefore, should be regarded as the means taken by God to allow for His merci- ful will to be carried out for His people, as revealed to Moses on Horeb; and it should also be regarded as the foundation of the Law given on Mount Sinai. The family sacrifice lay at the center of these two great revelations of God's mystery and joined them together. The sacrifice was offered at night in the bosom of the family, while the other two revelations took place on the mountaintops, in the brightness of the flame "that rose up from the midst of a bush," and on the mountain "wrapped in smoke, because the Lord descended upon it in fire" (Ex. 19:18-19; 24:16: "the glory of the Lord settled there on Mount Sinai, and the cloud covered it six days").

The revelation of the fatherly mercy of God for His people, the revelation of His hidden name, "the God who is," demanded from the people of Israel a fresh act of worship, allowing them to receive this mercy, to cooperate and participate in it. It was a loving, trustful, filial act of adoration, which called for God's answer, the new covenant of Mount Sinai:

> If you walk in my statutes and observe my commandments and do them, then I will give you your rains in their season, and the land shall yield its increase, and the trees of the field shall yield their fruit. And your threshing shall last to the time of vintage, and the vintage shall last to the time for sowing; and you shall eat your bread to the full, and dwell in your land securely. And I will give peace in the land, and you shall lie down, and none shall make you afraid; and I will remove evil beasts from the land, and the sword shall not go through your land. And you shall chase your enemies, and they shall fall before you by the sword. . . . And I will make my abode among you, and my soul shall not abhor you. And I will walk among you, and will be your God, and you shall be my people. I am the Lord your God, who brought you forth out of

the land of Egypt, that you should not be
their slaves; and I have broken the bars of
your yoke and made you walk erect" (Lev.
26:3-7, 11-13).

There is the opposite side of this covenant: "If you spurn
my statutes . . . I will send pestilence among you, and you
shall be delivered into the hand of the enemy" (Lev. 26:15-25).

By means of the Law of this covenant, God revealed His
holy rights to Moses and His people. He revealed to them His
jealousy and wisdom as lawgiver.

The Sacrifice of Elijah

The liturgy of the various sacrifices was extended and
more clearly laid down under the Law. It was a liturgy of
holocausts or burnt offerings, in which all was consumed to
declare God's sovereign rights, the supreme adoration of sacrifice (Lev. 1:1-17; Ex. 29:38, 46); a liturgy of the offering of
first fruits, to show God's rights over all fertility (Lev. 2:1-16);
a liturgy of welcome offerings or peace offerings, which
showed that God alone gives peace, for He is beyond all strife
(Lev. 3:1-17); a liturgy of sacrifices for sin, begging mercy
and forgiveness (Lev. 4:5-13); a liturgy of sacrifices of expiation, to make amends (Lev. 4:14-20). But the celebration of
the Passover (the feast of unleavened bread) always remained
the center of the whole Law—the supreme Sabbath with its
seven days of rest.

These positive laws, which determined in detail the
whole great liturgy of the people of Israel, codified in an
explicit form what already existed in such abundance. It is

unnecessary for our present purpose to pause over the different liturgies. They interest us only insofar as they show the particular finality of the different sacrifices: to worship the sovereign majesty of God, to implore His intervention, to recognize His absolute rights, to thank Him for His blessings, and to make reparation so far as we can. All these public religious acts, derived from the virtue of religion, demanded an inner activity, a moral intention of adoration, prayer, praise, and contrition. Otherwise these liturgies would be meaningless and would become hypocritical.

They would fall into religious legalism, a dreadful and hateful thing, since, in favor of what is external, it neglects what is most inward, hidden in the depth of man's heart, that is, his personal relation to his God. Men supposed they were worshiping God if they carried out a sacred rite of sacrifice, of burnt offering, if they fulfilled the material provisions of the Law. We know how Israel, and mankind in general, has often slipped into this dreadful fault. Then the rigorous, material practice of the Law kills its spirit.

Men supposed they were doing their duty when they offered the sacrifices demanded by the Law; the same attitude may be seen in the Christian today who thinks he has done his duty if he has been to Sunday Mass, even though during the Mass he has made no inward act of worship or love. The inward attitude seems of little importance; all that really matters is to fulfill the precept materially. What a hypocrite would the man be who deliberately acted thus! The prophets vigorously declaimed this fault, for such an attitude not only materializes worship, and utterly disfigures it by taking away all its nobility, but, at a deeper level, falsifies in man's spirit all true knowledge of God, regarding Him as a kind of manager who marks down the material presence or absence, without troubling about anything else. God is acknowledged as the One who "searches the mind and heart"; but the fact that He is a faithful and merciful God, demanding above all a loving heart, is totally forgotten. The Law was only a means for educating God's people and making them a religious people. Faced with this legalistic materialization of adoration, this low appreciation of God's mystery, the prophets never ceased to recall that the Lord demanded above all a contrite heart, a loving heart, an inward worship, directed to God as a spirit.

> What to me is the multitude of your sacrifices? says the Lord; I have had enough of burnt offerings of rams and the fat of fed beasts; I do not delight in the blood of bulls, or of lambs, or of he-goats. When you come to appear before me, who requires of you this trampling of my courts? Bring no more vain offerings; incense is an abomination to me. New moon and Sabbath and the calling of assemblies—I cannot endure iniquity and solemn assembly. Your new moons and your appointed feasts my soul hates; they have become a burden to me, I am weary of bearing them. When you spread forth your hands, I will hide my eyes from you; even though you make many prayers, I will not listen; your hands are full of blood. Wash yourselves; make

yourselves clean; remove the evil of your doings
from before my eyes (Is. 1:11-16).

I hate, I despise your feasts, and I take no
delight in your solemn assemblies. Even
though you offer me your burnt offerings and
cereal offerings, I will not accept them, and
the peace offerings of your fatted beasts I will
not look upon. Take away from me the noise
of your songs; to the melody of your harps I
will not listen (Amos 5:21-23).

They sacrifice flesh and eat it; but the Lord
has no delight in them (Hos. 8:13).

For I desire steadfast love and not sacrifice,
the knowledge of God, rather than burnt
offerings (Hos. 6:6).

The prophets often seem to express nostalgia for the
time of the wandering in the desert: Israel then worshiped
God with greater purity and sincerity of heart.

Although the prophets fought against this legalistic
formalism of a Law which was being understood materially
and recalled the supreme importance of moral intention, of
purity of heart and mind, we must not conclude that they
opposed the Law, or neglected or wished to do away with the
sacrifices that gave official, communal witness to Israel's
fidelity to its God. Worship of God had first to flow from the
hearts of the faithful, from that which was most inward and
spiritual in them, for it required an ever purer knowledge of
God's mystery. To be entire and complete, however, it had to

take possession of all their sensitive and physical life; it had to become outward and show itself. This was all the more necessary since the people of Israel lived amid peoples who worshiped false gods and idols. Israel was always tempted to imitate them and accept some of their beliefs. For this reason, God commanded them: "Take heed to yourself, lest you make a covenant with the inhabitants of the land whither you go, lest it become a snare in the midst of you . . . and when they play the harlot after their gods and sacrifice to their gods and one invites you, you eat of his sacrifice" (Ex. 34:12-15).

Moses and the prophets were to fight stubbornly against these temptations and contaminations which the Law condemned so plainly: "You shall not make gods of silver to be with me, nor shall you make for yourselves gods of gold" (Ex. 20:23).

We must not forget that Moses' first act when he came down from Mount Sinai and caught sight of the golden calf, the idol made by the people of Israel, "a stiff-necked race," was to break the tablets of the Law he was carrying, which he had just received from God—those tablets of stone on which the finger of God had written the Ten Commandments. This idolatrous people was no longer worthy to receive them because it had already broken the first commandment, on which all the others depended. In his holy anger, Moses "took the calf which they had made, and burnt it with fire, and ground it to powder, and scattered it upon the water, and made the people of Israel drink it" (Ex. 32:20).

The prophets never ceased proclaiming that the Lord was the true God and that the other gods were nothing, that idols had no power, and that the chosen people were called to give faithful witness to the Lord.

Only two passages need to be quoted; the first is from the prophet Hosea:

> When Ephraim spoke, men trembled; he was exalted in Israel; but he incurred guilt through Baal and died. And now they sin more and more, and make for themselves molten images, idols skillfully made of their silver, all of them the work of craftsmen. Sacrifice to these, they say. Men kiss calves! Therefore they shall be like the morning mist or like the dew that goes early away, like the chaff that swirls from the threshing floor or like smoke from a window. I am the Lord your God from the land of Egypt; you know no God but me, and besides me there is no savior (Hos. 13:1-4).

And Isaiah:

> You are my witnesses, says the Lord, and my servant whom I have chosen, that you may know and believe me and understand that I am He. Before me no god was formed, nor shall there be any after me. I, I am the Lord, and besides me there is no savior (Is. 43:10-11).

It is against this background of struggle to maintain in purity the worship of the Lord, the only true God, that we must see the unique sacrifice of the prophet Elijah, during the reign of Ahab, if we are to understand the fresh lesson it teaches.

At the request of Elijah, Ahab summoned all Israel to Mount Carmel, as well as the 450 prophets of Baal and the 400 prophets of the forest shrines who sat at the table of Jezebel. Then Elijah went before all the people, and said:

> How long will you go limping with two different opinions? If the Lord is God, follow him; but if Baal, then follow him. And the people did not answer him a word. Then Elijah said to the people, "I, even I only, am left a prophet of the Lord; but Baal's prophets are four hundred and fifty men. Let two bulls be given to us; and let them choose one bull for themselves, and cut it in pieces and lay it on the wood, but put no fire to it; and I will prepare the other bull and lay it on the wood, and put no fire to it. And you call on the name of your god and I will call on the name of the Lord; and the God who answers by fire, he is God" (1 Kings 18:21-24).

Elijah's intention is clear. He appeals to the omnipotence of God, that God may show by a miracle that He alone is the true God. The situation is so tragic and hopeless from a human point of view that Elijah does not hesitate to call for this extraordinary means, which directly implicates God. The whole people approve what the prophet proposed. Were not the prophets of Baal, to whom Elijah grants precedence, more numerous? After choosing a bull and preparing it, they invoked the name of Baal:

And they took the bull which was given them, and they prepared it, and called on the name of Baal from morning until noon, saying, "O Baal, answer us!" But there was no voice, and no one answered. And they limped about the altar which they had made. And at noon Elijah mocked them, saying, "Cry aloud, for he is a god; either he is musing, or he has gone aside, or he is on a journey, or perhaps he is asleep and must be awakened." And they cried aloud, and cut themselves after their custom with swords and lances, until the blood gushed out upon them. And as midday passed, they raved on until the time of the offering of the oblation, but there was no voice; no one answered, no one heeded.

Then Elijah said to all the people, "Come near to me"; and all the people came near to him. And he repaired the altar of the Lord that had been thrown down; Elijah took twelve stones, according to the number of the tribes of the sons of Jacob, to whom the word of the Lord came, saying, "Israel shall be your name"; and with the stones he built an altar in the name of the Lord. And he made a trench about the altar, as great as would contain two measures of seed. And he put the wood in order, and cut the bull in pieces and laid it on the wood. And he said, "Fill four jars with water, and pour it on the burnt

offering, and on the wood." And he said, "Do
it a second time"; and they did it a second
time. And he said, "Do it a third time"; and
they did it a third time. And the water ran
round about the altar, and filled the trench also
with water.

And at the time of the offering of the oblation, Elijah the prophet came near and said,
"O Lord, God of Abraham, Isaac, and Israel,
let it be known this day that thou art God in
Israel, and that I am thy servant, and that I
have done all these things at thy word.
Answer me, O Lord, answer me, that this people may know that thou hast turned their
hearts back." Then the fire of the Lord fell, and
consumed the burnt offering, and the wood,
and the stones, and the dust, and licked up
the water that was in the trench. And when all
the people saw it, they fell on their faces; and
they said, "The Lord, he is God; the Lord, he
is God." (1 Kings 18:26-39).

Among the sacrifices codified by the Law, Elijah's sacrifice here, which appeals to the omnipotence of God for its
fulfillment, seems entirely unique. It is an apologetic sacrifice
in the strictest sense, a divine apologetic: God intervening
miraculously to awaken a faith that was weak and asleep.

The miraculous fire that came down from Heaven at the
prayer of Elijah not only showed the power of God's presence, His fatherly care, and the absolute transcendence of the

true God, who alone is worthy of worship and sacrifice, but also His overflowing love and His devouring presence. For He showed Himself under the form of a devouring fire that not only consumed the victim prepared upon the wood, but took possession of everything, devouring even what should have quenched it, the water around the altar.

This sacrifice was offered on Mount Carmel and not within the precincts of the Temple, since it was offered in the course of a struggle and in front of all the prophets of Baal— Elijah being the only prophet of the Lord. This sacrifice of struggle and victory appears all the greater from its simplicity of form. Only what is essential is retained. But the essential aspect of this sacrifice unfolds in an opposite order than the other sacrifices. Ordinarily, the sacrifice of burnt offering expresses the inward act of adoration. The inward act comes first and gives meaning to the outward acts, the sacrifice of the victim and its destruction. In this case, the outward acts are first laid down as purely external acts, the conventional rite, involving no sacrifice. Elijah would not have had the right to tell the prophets of Baal to offer their idolatrous sacrifice, but he could tell them to perform outward acts and await the judgment of God, signified by the descent of the fire, in order to bring about the inward act of adoration. This sacrifice is wonderfully instructive. It shows emphatically that outward acts in themselves have no sacrificial power; they only perform a particular action. They are in the order of doing something. These outward acts are sacrifices only if they express and signify an inward act of adoration, an act by which we acknowledge the sovereign majesty of God our Creator and our Father, on whom we depend absolutely for all that we are. For this reason, an act of adoration of this kind can be directed only toward the one true God. To direct it toward a "Baal," who does not exist, is to waste our time. It is to deceive ourselves and others if the false act of worship is translated into outward acts of sacrifice.

The sacrifice of Elijah shows, too, the close bonds that unite prayer of petition and adoration. In some sense, the prayer that surrounded this sacrifice was as an attitude of soul far less determined than adoration. Nevertheless, in its true character, prayer means that we express to God all our desires and all our distress; it is the request of one who has nothing, of the poor man who reveals his needs to Him who relieves them, who can help.[8]

Through adoration, we are motionless in God's presence; adoration makes us nothing in the presence of God. We disappear as one who is nothing before Him who is.[9]

---

8. Expressions such as: "Yet have regard to the prayer of thy servant and to his supplication, O Lord my God, hearkening to the cry and to the prayer which thy servant prays before thee this day; . . . hear thou in heaven thy dwelling place; and when thou hearest, forgive" (1 Kings 8:28, 30) are extremely significant. We find them in all the great prayers of Scripture and in the promises.

9. The following passage from the book of Joshua is very significant. "When Joshua was by Jericho, he lifted up his eyes and looked, and behold, a man stood before him with his drawn sword in his hand; and Joshua went to him and said, 'Are you for us, or for our adversaries?' And he said, 'No; but as commander of the army of the Lord I have now come.' And Joshua fell on his face to the earth, and worshiped, and said to him, 'What does my lord bid his servant?' And the commander of the Lord's army said to Joshua, 'Put off your shoes from your feet; for the place where you stand is holy.' And Joshua did so" (Josh. 5:13-15).

Prayer is an appeal, a cry to God, who can seem to remain quite distant. Adoration has far greater depth. It leaves everything to God. Prayer has a more subjective and affective character.[10]

It is by means of prayer that Elijah obtained his desire for the fire to come down on the victim. His prayer expressed the apostolic desire of his heart. He felt so strongly the lack of faith in the people of God, the extreme peril in which they stood. The fire from Heaven caused all those present to adore. The sudden presence of God, shown symbolically by the fire, called forth at once an act of adoration.

The sacrifice of Elijah possessed a wonderful efficacy from the very fact that it was God Himself who replied, intervened, and manifested His overwhelming love by a miraculous fire. The sacrifice immediately caused an act of adoration. All the people were seized with fear and fell with their faces to the ground, acknowledging that it is the Lord who is God. It converted the hearts of those present, declaring the truth of their faith in the Lord, the only true God, heightening their sense of the presence of the Almighty and of the efficacy of His jealousy: the fire consumed even the water.

This miraculous sacrifice is the great manifestation of the one, incomparable God, who watches jealously over His people and His prophets, who loves them as their friend, replying at once to their prayer.

---

10. It may be said that contemplation is a conversation between friends, when he whom God calls is present to his God. It is also a struggle in a rivalry of love, and, finally, it is the silent presence of love.

The Sacrifice of the Seven Brothers and of Their Mother

Finally, in quite a different context, and at a far later period, we should notice these last sacrifices, which yet possess remarkable features.[11]

The many martyrdoms mentioned in the book of Maccabees should be referred to, but we may consider as especially significant that of the seven brothers and of their mother in the reign of Antiochus Epiphanes, which was held in such honor by early Christian tradition.[12]

These seven brothers and their mother, one after the other, chose to suffer torture and death rather than to break the Law given to their fathers, each of them declaring with utmost resolution: "We are ready to die rather than transgress the laws of our fathers" (2 Mac. 7:2); "I got these [his tongue and his hands] from Heaven, and because of his laws I disdain them, and from him I hope to get them back again" (2 Mac. 7:11); "One cannot but choose to die at the hands of men and to cherish the hope that God gives of being raised again by him" (2 Mac. 7:14).

The youngest, whom Antiochus especially tried to win over, promising to make him his friend and grant him high

---

11. The occasion was the struggle against the Seleucids to gain the religious and political freedom of the Jewish people. The chief hero of this story is Judas Maccabeus, whose father, Mattathias, had urged on the holy war against Antiochus Epiphanes, who profaned the Temple and began the persecution.

12. Churches were dedicated to them at Antioch, Rome, Lyons, and Vienne.

office if he agreed to abandon the traditions of his fathers (2 Mac. 7:24), remained unmoved by such offers and persuasions: "What are you waiting for? I will not obey the king's command, but I obey the command of the law that was given to our fathers through Moses" (2 Mac. 7:30).

Their mother, seeing her seven sons die in a single day, "bore it with good courage because of her hope in the Lord. . . . Filled with a noble spirit, she fired her woman's reasoning with a man's courage" (2 Mac. 7:20-21). She reminded them of the sovereign rights of the Creator, especially over "the breath of life," and His almighty mercy, which should help them to despise themselves for the love of God's laws.

Her character shows itself more clearly in her attitude toward her youngest son. The king wished to make use of her to tempt the boy by a promise to save his life.

> After much urging on his part, she undertook to persuade her son. But, leaning close to him, she spoke in their native tongue as follows, deriding the cruel tyrant: "My son, have pity on me. I carried you nine months in my womb, nursed you for three years, and have reared you and brought you up to this point in your life, and have taken care of you. I beseech you, my child, to look at the heaven and the earth and see everything that is in them, and recognize that God did not make them out of things that existed. Thus also mankind comes into being. Do not fear this

butcher, but prove worthy of your brothers.
Accept death, so that in God's mercy I may
get you back again with your brothers." . . .
Last of all, the mother died, after her sons
(2 Mac. 7:26-29, 41).

By this martyrdom, which is sacrifice in the truest sense,
these brothers and their mother not only gave witness to their
living faith in the omnipotence of the Creator, who sees all
things and on whom all things depend; but, at a deeper level,
they declared their absolute trust and their hope in the mercy
of their God, who has compassion and will raise them up to
eternal life.

By their martyrdom, which was freely accepted, they
acknowledged that their earthly life had meaning only in reference to eternal life. So, too, they witnessed that God alone
is the source of life, and for Him death does not exist.

While the sacrifice of Elijah bore witness to the truth of
the one God, calling directly upon His omnipotence, here the
witness is of a different nature. It is given by "sons of God,"
who, owing to a special assistance from divine mercy, have
been given the power to endure without faltering the tor-
ments of a bloody death, allowing them to remain faithful to
the laws of their fathers to the end. The efficacious help
granted them by God's omnipotence is here entirely within.
It is upon the hearts of these brothers and of their mother
that the fire from Heaven comes down and brings about that
heroic act of obedience involving their death. Hence, this sacrifice calls for an act of intimate adoration within the act of
obedience, lived in love—an act of adoration that allowed

these brothers and their mother to regard their lives as nothing, to "despise" them before the almighty mercy of their God and the exacting requirements of His Law. The outward martyrdom, the tortures and death, express the inward act by which they offered up their lives to their God. They offered themselves freely to God, recognizing that He alone is God, that the law expressing His will is holy, and that it must be observed even if this requires the sacrifice of their lives.

This inward act of adoration has a special character of reparation. They are willing to offer their lives in order to make amends for the sins of the people of Israel, of whom they are members, and with whom they acknowledge being in solidarity:

> "Do not deceive yourself in vain," said the sixth son to Antiochus, "for we are suffering these things on our own account, because of our sins against our own God" (2 Mac. 7:18). The youngest cried out: "For we are suffering because of our own sins. . . . I, like my brothers, give up body and life for the laws of our fathers, appealing to God to show mercy soon to our nation and by afflictions and plagues to make you confess that He alone is God, and through me and my brothers to bring to an end the wrath of the Almighty which has just fallen on our whole nation" (2 Mac. 7:32, 37-38).

This act of adoration, then, called in a special way for God's mercy, His saving mercy, which has compassion and grants pardon, while at the same time it called for His justice, which punished them for their sins and would punish Antiochus later on. This is emphasized by the brothers when, about to suffer, they said to Antiochus:

> "But do not think that you will go unpunished for having tried to fight against God!" (2 Mac. 7:19).

> "Keep on, and see how his mighty power will torture you and your descendants!" (2 Mac. 7:17).

> "But you, who have contrived all sorts of evil against the Hebrews, will certainly not escape the hands of God" (2 Mac. 7:31).

> "You, by the judgment of God, will receive just punishment for your arrogance" (2 Mac. 7:36).

This act of worship, inspired by great hope, was wholly directed toward eternal life and heavenly contemplation. It was a direct entryway to the vision of God and a strong call for the resurrection of the body. "I got these from Heaven, and because of his laws I disdain them, and from him I hope to get them back again" (2 Mac. 7:11). The youngest expressed this great hope: "For our brothers after enduring a brief suffering have drunk of everflowing life under God's covenant!" (2 Mac. 7:36).

As martyrdom, this sacrifice possesses a unique reality and value, not merely as an inward act of living faith, nor merely as an act of obedience like that of Abraham, but as the fulfillment of an act that required a gift of the whole self, consummated in death. This sacrifice is, therefore, "prefigurative" of the sacrifice of Christ on the Cross in a deeper sense than the sacrifices previously mentioned. In its very reality, it has a close relation to the martyrdom of Christ, which it foretells in a most striking and explicit way. It may be said to be the final preparation for Christ's sacrifice. That is why it makes such a deep impression on us.

The martyrdom of the mother, who joined her seven sons and cooperated in their sacrifice, particularly in that of the youngest, gives an extraordinary richness to this sacrifice. The mother assisted actively in the martyrdom of her sons, helping them as a mother should, comforting them, encouraging them "in her own native tongue" (it is a mother who preserves the living language and traditions and hands them on to her children). She herself died in silence. The prefiguration of Mary present at the foot of the Cross, at Christ's martyrdom, urging her "youngest son" to be faithful to the example of the Elder Son, is remarkable.

This sacrifice, calling upon God's mercy, possesses a superabundance, a fullness, of mercy. It gives access to the final covenant with God. And since it implies the gift of present life, surrendered to God in order to glorify Him, God's answer can only be the gift of glory: "the King of the universe will raise us up to an everlasting renewal of life" (2 Mac. 7:9). It is by a sacrifice of martyrdom that the final promise of the covenant, the mystery of what lies beyond, is revealed to us explicitly and for the first time.

Obedience to the Law led to martyrdom. In the case of these seven brothers and their mother, the Law—given to

God's people as a divine means for their education to make
of them a religious people consecrated to God—attained its
end in an ultimate and wonderfully efficacious fashion. The
first commandment, to worship God, was carried out fully in
this martyrdom.

* * *

These six great acts of sacrificial worship each have their
own power and, hence, reach a wonderful completeness,
showing us progressively the mystery of the almighty mercy
of the Lord, the mystery of the creative omnipotence of the
Father, the mystery of unfathomable wisdom and fidelity.

These six acts of sacrificial worship demand on man's
side the exercise of his religious activity; the exercise of his
theological faith, hope, and charity; and the exercise of obedience and penance. They make man put into practice what
is deepest and most personal in him, and deepest, too, in his
whole communal life and social functions, and in his capacity to make use of all the fruits of the earth and of animals.

These six sacrifices, while perfect in themselves, still
remain prefigurations of Christ's sacrifice of adoration. They
derive their full meaning and value from the sacrifice of
Christ.

CHAPTER 2

THE SACRIFICE OF ADORATION
ON THE CROSS

THE MYSTERY OF CHRIST CRUCIFIED

THE sacrifice of the Cross completes all the sacrifices of the Old Testament, giving them their finality and containing in a more eminent way all their perfections. This sacrifice is incomparably greater and more profound than those of the Old Testament; it is the supreme sacrifice, because it is that of the Man-God, of the Incarnate Word, who came into this world to accomplish it. Nevertheless, to the Christian, the sacrifices of the Old Testament should be ways to approach the sacrifice of Christ, giving us an imperfect yet true and divine outline, as it were, of this supreme mystery.[13]

We should not neglect what God deigned to teach us, in His divine pedagogy, to enable us to understand more fully the mystery of the Cross. Therefore, before considering the mystery in and of itself and its most unique and original

---

13. Cf. 1 Cor. 10:11: "When all this happened to them, it was a symbol."

qualities, let us consider how each one of these rough approaches tells us one aspect of the mystery.

Like the sacrifice of the seven brothers and of their mother, Christ's sacrifice, too, is a martyrdom of an only Son and His Mother. Jesus completed His earthly life with the torture and Crucifixion in order to remain faithful to what the will of His Father required of Him. The sacrifice of the Cross, too, is accomplished in an act of obedience. It remains a witness of Christ's faithful attachment to the will of His Father. The sacrifice of the Cross, too, is an act of adoration that makes amends for the sins of the people of Israel. Jesus offers Himself to the Father as bearing the responsibility for all sinful mankind, answering before the justice of the Father for the iniquity of the world. He is the Lamb of God, who bears the sins of the world. Christ's sacrifice is a pledge of eternal life. It opens Heaven and makes possible our entry into the Kingdom of God. It is inseparable from the mystery of the Resurrection, of glory. Hence it is that to St. John the mystery of the Cross is the glorification of the Father. Mary is silently present. She is given to the youngest of the apostles to help him remain faithful to the end.

Like the sacrifice of Elijah, the sacrifice of the Cross, joined to the mystery of the Resurrection, is the supreme sign of Christ's divinity, of the true divinity of Him who sent Him. It is the only sign Christ gave, a sign symbolized in the Old Testament by the prophet Jonah, who remained for three days in the belly of the whale. The sacrifice of the Cross is a sacrifice that is carried out by the breath of love, the fire from Heaven that comes down and consumes the whole victim. Jesus Himself gave up His soul at the moment willed by the

Father, when the Father (in His soul) took Him to Himself. When men nailed Christ to the wood of the Cross, He showed by His sacrifice and Resurrection that He had indeed been sent by the one God. The sacrifice of Christ on the hill of Calvary was accomplished after a contest in which Jesus overcame Lucifer. He unmasked the kingdom of the Prince of this world.

Christ crucified is our Passover, the true Passover, the "passing by" of God, who delivers us from the yoke of slavery to sin and who leads us through the "desert" to the "promised land," to the land of life, our heavenly home, to glory.

Before the Cross came the Last Supper, and this continues for us in the mystery of the Eucharist, that divine, family meal by which we are fed on the flesh of the Lamb who has been sacrificed.

The sacrifice of the Cross is the offering of the true Isaac, the "child of promise," immolated as the son of promise and as the "scapegoat" taken from the thicket. This theological sacrifice, carried out wholly in obedience to the will of the Father, expresses the loving choice of Jesus for His Father. Jesus knew that He was crucifying the heart of His Mother when He accepted the mysterious will of His Father. He knew that He was crucifying His beloved disciples and drawing them to Himself, the Crucified One, to allow them to be with Him, and in Him to be crucified. He was prepared to drink the chalice that His Father willed Him to drink—"not my will, but thine, be done," He said in His prayer to the Father in the Agony in the Garden (Lk. 22:42).

The sacrifice of the Cross is the simplest and most perfect of the acts of sacrifice, or of offering, or of thanksgiving, purer than that of Abel, more perfect than the thanksgiving of Noah. By offering His body as a victim of love and worship, He offered to the Father the first-fruits of all humanity, the most excellent and wonderful thing produced by the world. He offered to the Father an utterly pure victim.

The chief priests and Pharisees decided on His death out of fraternal and religious jealousy. Did He not blasphemously claim to be the son of God? Had He not violated the law of the Sabbath?

While the sacrifice of the Cross gathered together in itself all the perfections of the sacrifices of the Old Testament that prefigured it, it was also carried out in a more eminent way. What the types could not express (because they were only types and, as such, could not proclaim what types cannot give), the mystery of Christ crucified carried out and gave us: the sacrifice of the well-beloved Son of the Father giving Himself to us as our Savior.

None of the perfections discovered and acknowledged in the types disappeared, but all were changed in this final consummation, the masterpiece of God's wisdom. The sacrifice of the Cross is above all the sacrifice of love, the love of the Son for the Father and of the Father for the Son, the love of the Father for us and of the Son for us, a love that is revealed to us and granted to us. It is the gift of the well-beloved Son that is made to us on the Cross. The mystery of the Eucharist bears witness to it and communicates it to us, and indeed, to every man who is redeemed by the blood of Christ. The

Cross is the great revelation of love for us, in that new worship "in spirit and truth," accomplished by the Son. Or, if one prefers, it is a loving worship which wholly takes possession of Christ and reveals to us His love for the Father and for us, and the love of the Father for Him and for us.

These two aspects, worship in spirit and in truth, manifesting the mystery of love, are inseparable, but we have to distinguish them in order to explain them as clearly as possible.

The Mystery of the Cross: Worship in Spirit and in Truth

The mystery of the Cross is essentially a holocaust of filial adoration, of reparation and satisfaction. St. Paul tells us plainly: "Therefore be imitators of God, as beloved children. And walk in love, as Christ loved us and gave himself up for us, a fragrant offering and sacrifice to God" (Eph. 5:1-2; cf. Ps. 40:6; Gal. 2:20). It is this supreme sacrifice which glorifies the Father, effecting the most profound, true, and filial adoration possible.

Our Lord did not come to abolish the Law but to fulfill it, to give it its final significance and efficacy. Since the whole Law, as we have seen, is rooted in the first commandment, to worship God and Him alone, it follows that Jesus, the supreme "servant of the Lord," alone lived in a singular way in accordance with the first commandment of the Law. He lived with such intensity of love that He transformed the Law, giving it a far deeper and more divine meaning: the worship of a servant for his master was changed into the worship of the well-beloved Son for His Father. It is on the Cross that is accomplished and shown in full all that filial worship should be—a worship that Jesus never ceased to carry out throughout His whole life. The Epistle to the Hebrews states clearly: "Consequently, when Christ came into the world, he said, 'Sacrifices and offerings thou hast not desired, but a body hast thou prepared for me; in burnt offerings and sin offerings thou hast taken no pleasure.' Then I said, 'Lo, I have come to do thy will, O God,' as it is written of me in the roll of the book.' " And the author of the Epistle to the Hebrews adds: "He abolishes the first in order to establish the second" (Heb. 10:5-9; cf. Ps. 40:7-9). The mystery of the Cross, which is completed by the piercing with the lance, shows us this clearly.

To understand the change in the first commandment of the Law, to grasp the distinction between adoration in the Gospel and adoration in the Old Testament, we should consider the religious attitude of Christ, His prayer of adoration to the Father throughout the Gospels and, above all, on the Cross. We should observe, especially in the Gospels of St. Luke and St. John, that deep inclination of Jesus' soul for the solitude of the desert and the mountains in order to give Himself up more fully to the prayer of adoration (Lk. 6:12; Jn. 6:15).

Undoubtedly, Jesus had no need of solitude in order to pray; He prayed to His Father always. But He wished to show us the need to leave all that is not God, to find Him more perfectly, and pray to Him more fervently.

Here I need only mention certain passages in which Jesus gives His teaching with special emphasis. When the Samaritan woman says to Him: "Our fathers worshiped on this mountain, and you say that in Jerusalem is the place where men ought to worship," Jesus teaches distinctly: "Woman, believe me, the hour is coming, when neither on this mountain nor in Jerusalem will you worship the Father. . . . But the hour is coming, and now is, when the true worshipers will worship the Father in spirit and truth, for such the Father seeks to worship him. God is spirit, and those who worship him must worship in spirit and truth" (Jn. 4:20-21, 23).

The whole ritual dimension of religious adoration always runs the risk of materializing what is purest and most delicate in man's heart, his call toward God, his desire to worship Him, by engrossing his attention with external details, physical actions, and movements to the detriment of what is essential, namely, inner intention. The ritual aspect is transcended by Jesus—not despised, but treated as quite secondary. The emphasis is on inner adoration. Jesus accomplished what the prophets had already outlined.

Inner adoration is described as worship "in spirit." It is worship which comes from the Spirit, which is carried out in the spirit of love, worship which must spring from love and take possession of all that is deepest in the soul.

It is worship "in truth"; it must be directed to the one true God and must be carried out with an ever clearer and firmer faith, which distinguishes plainly between the mystery of God and all that is not God.

To grasp what the meaning of the interiority of adoration implies, we should compare the other passages in the Gospels in which our Lord demands from us interior prayer:

> And when you pray, you must not be like the
> hypocrites; for they love to stand and pray

in the synagogues and at the street corners,
that they may be seen by men. Truly, I say to
you, they have their reward. But when you
pray, go into your room and shut the door
and pray to your Father who is in secret; and
your Father who sees in secret will reward you
(Mt. 6:5-6).

And in praying do not heap up empty
phrases as the Gentiles do; for they think that
they will be heard for their many words. Do
not be like them, for your Father knows what
you need before you ask him. Pray then like
this: Our Father who art in heaven, hallowed
be thy name. Thy kingdom come, thy will be
done, on earth as it is in heaven (Mt. 6:7-10).

Yet we should not suppose that prayer, if it is good
prayer, should be merely occasional. Jesus says the opposite: "And he told them a parable, to the effect that they
ought always to pray and not lose heart" (Lk. 18:1). We
know, too, the parable of the importunate friend (Lk. 11:5
ff.). We must knock and never cease knocking until the door
opens, and this demands very great filial confidence. We can
only pray inwardly, unceasingly, without giving up, if we
possess an entire confidence through every trial (cf.
Gen. 19:17-25).

The confidence of a friend and a son cannot exist without genuine poverty of spirit and humility. Prayer, if it is to
be effective, must flow from a humble and contrite heart, for
otherwise it loses all meaning. To tell God of our merits and

title to glory is not to pray, as we are shown in the parable of the Pharisee and the publican (Lk. 18:9-14).

What has been said of prayer is still truer of adoration, which should embody the more hidden and profound elements of prayer. It is this loving filial worship which dwells in the heart of Jesus throughout the mystery of the Cross. This mystery begins with the prayer of the Agony, which is a prayer offered in private. Jesus was alone, without witnesses; for even the most faithful apostles fell asleep despite Jesus' advice: "Pray that you may not enter into temptation" (Lk. 22:40). Jesus says to His Father: "Remove this cup from me; nevertheless not my will, but thine, be done" (Lk. 22:42).

He lays bear to His Father the most natural and spontaneous desire of His heart. And in so doing, He leaves the matter entirely to the Father's good pleasure. Jesus offers the Father His desires and leaves Him to do as He wishes. Here is the inward sacrifice of the soul, beginning in a wholly hidden fashion. This offering is the loving adoration of the Son, who presents Himself to His Father, surrendering Himself wholly into His hands, telling Him of His most burning desires, but at the same time offering them up to Him. The loving and filial adoration during the Agony utterly prostrates Him: "And being in an agony he prayed more earnestly; and his sweat became like great drops of blood falling down upon the ground" (Lk. 22:44).

This interior adoration continues throughout the bloody sacrifice of the Crucifixion; Christ worships His Father in the silence of His heart, worshiping in spirit and truth. He worships Him in the humility and extreme poverty of one who is rejected and condemned by His religious community. This

adoration in spirit and truth is expressed with His whole
nature, His whole body. Worship in spirit and truth does not
mean angelic worship, exclusively spiritual, without any outward manifestation; but the most essential aspect of worship
in spirit and truth is its inner, hidden, silent, and loving quality. Precisely since it is an adoration of love alone, it needs to
be real in a very high degree. It must be carried out even in the
body of the man who worships God; he must also be the
victim sacrificed and offered. When interior adoration is
expressed symbolically by means of an outward victim, an ani-
mal such as a lamb, it always remains "intentional" in the one
adoring. When adoration is the fruit of love and entirely
determined by love, this "intentional mode" and symbolic
expression are repugnant to the realism of love.

Adoration such as this cannot be satisfied with remaining in signs and intentionality. It strives to reach the thing
loved directly in itself, and for this reason, true worship, fruit
of love, cannot be satisfied with symbolic expression. It seeks
to become real in the most effective way. The filial, entirely
loving, adoration of His Father in the soul of Jesus was
expressed in His own body, offered as the victim of the holocaust and, ultimately and supremely, in His heart. By His willingness to let His own body be scourged and crucified, He was
able to offer it to the Father in a holocaust of adoration. His
body was the most precious and excellent thing in the whole
world, and thus He proclaimed officially the absolute rights of
God over all humanity and the whole world.

This sacrifice of adoration is also a sacrifice of reparation
for the sins of the human race. Christ on the Cross made satisfaction for the sins of the human race. He was the "Lamb of

God," bearing all the sins of the world. He was the "scape-goat," freely accepting to take upon Himself the shame of all His people, of all mankind. He wished to appear before His Father as solely responsible for the sins of men—even for the sin of the traitor Judas. Christ offers to the Father His blood-stained body, all the wounds from His scourging, all the pains of His Crucifixion, all the inner sadness of the Agony in the Garden, in order to win forgiveness for our sins.

Hence it is that the sacrifice of the Cross shows us the wonderful mercy of Christ for us, while at the same time revealing the mystery of the justice and mercy of the Father.

All the actions of the apostolic life of Christ the Good Shepherd were plainly acts of mercy to His sheep, to all men. But it is in the Agony in the Garden and on the Cross that we really reach the mystery of His merciful heart.

All the sufferings of human sinners, all the conse-quences of sin, He made His own, accepting them freely. No suffering of mankind remained foreign to His heart; He knew them all and bore them all deep within His heart. Liv-ing with greater intensity than any other man, He bore them in His measureless love for each one of us. Suffering is pro-portionate to love, and hence it is so amazing that His mercy should be such as it is. He knew what He was doing. Being the Good Shepherd who knew His sheep with their weak-ness and needs, He knew that to be the Good Shepherd of men, with all that this involved, was to love the life of His sheep more than His own life, to be willing to put Him-self in the place of sinners, to be an outcast for the sake of His brethren, to be reduced to nothing, to be wretched, despised, and rejected beyond all others. The sacrifice of the

Cross, taking place in the particular circumstances in which it took place, shows well this fullness of mercy. Nothing was withheld; He accepted all the sufferings, all the humiliations, all the emptiness; He could go no lower.

Mercy consists not only in stretching out one's hand to help the weak, but also in bending down, like a mother, toward one who is fallen, descending lower than he in order to help him, taking him up, and giving him back his life. Christ was willing to be thought more wicked than Barabbas, a public sinner, a blasphemer, an enemy to the Law of Moses who did not observe the Sabbath, a dangerous man who stirred up the people. He was willing to be "as one from whom men hide their faces" (Is. 53:3), such that after death, His body was not respected, His side was opened, and His heart pierced.

Thus, the realism of His mercy extended over His whole being: no part of His body remaining unharmed and His soul experiencing the deadly sadness of the Agony.

In the sacrifice on the Cross, there is, therefore, supreme worship and supreme mercy. In the heart of Jesus crucified, filial worship was far from preventing His heart from attending to His brethren; on the contrary, it allowed Him, desiring as He did to help and comfort them, to be the true Savior of His brethren by bearing their sins and making reparation for them and giving them a new life.

We are told this plainly in the Epistle to the Hebrews: "For by a single offering he has perfected for all time those who are sanctified. And the Holy Spirit also bears witness to us; for after saying, 'This is the covenant that I will make with them after those days, says the Lord: I will put my laws on their hearts, and write them on their minds,' then he adds, 'I will remember their sins and their misdeeds no more.' Where there is forgiveness of these, there is no longer any offering for sin" (Heb. 10:14-18). The sacrifices of the Passover, of Elijah, of Abraham, and of Noah are eminently united.

In the Gospel, our Lord warned us that a legalistic and pharisaic attitude in religion could easily be the very contrary of an attitude of mercy. We should remember the parable of the Good Samaritan (Lk. 10:29 ff.). Finding a man by the roadside, half-dead, stripped and beaten by robbers, the priest and the Levite reveal themselves by their actions: seeing the man, they passed by on the other side.

We know from experience that it is easy to feel a certain psychological conflict between these two extreme attitudes. It is easy to contrast a religious attitude with a merciful attitude. The religious man is separated from his fellows in order to be devoted to divine worship alone, to the praise of God. The merciful man, on the other hand, is wholly concerned with men's sufferings. The former is hidden by the majesty of God; worshiping Him, he makes himself as nothing before God, and God alone absorbs his attention. The latter is lost amid his disinherited brethren, and the more they are disinherited, the more he desires to be with them and the more they have a right to his help and presence.

The merciful man hears only the voice of the poor, the cries of the suffering, and the heart-rending pleas of the dying. We could continue describing this kind of psychological conflict at length. We have all experienced it in some degree, and sometimes it becomes keenest among the more generous men and Christians.

Christ crucified carried out on the Cross the most loving and most religious adoration possible; and, at the same
time, as the Lamb of God bearing the sins of the world, He
accomplished the supreme act of mercy. In His heart, adoration and mercy were united in the fullness of charity.

The psychological conflicts are indeed left entirely behind,
absorbed by love. Christ's mercy on the Cross consists above
all in pardoning sinners, in making reparation, in giving satisfaction in their name. Now, sin, in its most mysterious aspect,
is an offense against the sovereign majesty of God. Hence, in
order to satisfy for sin, the absolute rights of the sovereign
majesty of God must be acknowledged, and this can fully be
done only in a sacrifice of adoration in which the whole
victim is offered and consumed in order to declare the
grandeur of God.

Further, above all, sin is pride, leading to disobedience,
revolt against the law and the will of God. When revolt fully
develops and is all-embracing, it turns into a declaration of
atheism. Then man, in order to be first, puts himself in God's
place, calling himself his own master, depending on no one
but himself. Instead of worshiping God and serving Him,
man worships man and serves himself, denying God, killing
Him in his heart and mind.

In order to make reparation for this atheism and idola-
try, the ultimate forms of human pride, the Son of Man freely
agreed, through love for men and in order to glorify the Father,
to lower Himself into nothingness in the depths of His heart
and mind—the mystery of the Agony—and this annihilation
of self became concrete in His flesh and finally pierced His
heart. To satisfy for the exaltation of the "superman," who

desires his absolute independence and total freedom, the true King of men—the perfect man, wisest of all, man fully man—had to accept responsibility for His brethren and had to choose the freedom of the Father before His own freedom, however lawful and natural.

Now, the adoration of Christ on the Cross involves the complete annihilation of the human heart and intelligence of Christ through an act of obedience. Hence, to the extent that Christ on the Cross worshiped His Father and offered Himself to Him as a sacrifice in humble obedience, He could satisfy and make amends for all His brethren who were sinners. It was in order to satisfy and make reparation for sinners that He lived through the adoration of the Agony and of the Cross. What is true of the satisfaction made for the sins of men, as offenses against the Father, is true of the mercy shown toward all the consequences of the sin.

Christ "the Good Shepherd" knows the sufferings of all men and has made all of them His own, taking them into His own heart as His own sufferings. He teaches us to make use of this as a means for greater love of the Father. Poverty, accepted as a punishment from God for our correction, can be a wonderful means to make us love Him more, to make us live in more complete obedience to Him. On the Cross, Jesus was the first to make use of these human sufferings; He accepted them in order to call down the Father's mercy more abundantly on all mankind and on all the Church. Jesus made use of these sufferings, which resulted from sin, as a means to beg His Father's help more urgently—is He not our Advocate on the Cross?—to lower Himself further into nothingness, in a more visible and explicit way, and to surrender

Himself still more fully. He surrenders Himself as the most wretched and deprived of men. He made Himself nothing before the majesty of the Father, as the poorest, most despised, most humiliated of men.

Christ crucified, the merciful Good Shepherd, is anxious for the safety of His sheep; He sympathizes to the full with their lot and carries the injured sheep upon His blood-stained shoulders.

This mercy, far from contradicting the religious attitude of worship which is wholly directed toward the majesty of the Father, is joined to it and makes it more intense. For He suffers with His sheep, communicating to them salvation and love of the Father, in order to let this love consume all and take hold of all. It is in order to associate truly His sheep with His act of adoration and of sacrifice, it is in order that they may glorify the Father, that He shows such mercy to them. Christ's act of mercy is an act that does not stop at relieving the material sufferings of men, at getting rid of their punishment; it is not merely philanthropy, but divine mercy, which rises up to God and to His love. For this reason, the apparent contradictions between acts of religion and acts of mercy disappear and are transcended. Jesus comforts and helps His sheep as the "Good Shepherd," with wonderful mercy and tenderness, in order to save them and bring them into the closest union of love with the Father, to bring them into the presence of the Father, and so that they may bring themselves into the Father's presence, with Him and in Him, that they may unite themselves with His filial adoration, His sacrifice of holocaust. Mercy allows His act of adoration to extend very far and to reach the heart of every man, bringing them all to the "narrow gate" and into the Father's house.

We can say, too, that the loving worship of Christ crucified, a filial adoration "in spirit and truth," unites Him so closely to the almighty mercy of God that it allows the heart of Jesus to be a living source of mercy. The more we are united to God, the more we can live like God, according to His ways. The higher we are raised in love of God and the more willing we are to descend deeply into our littleness in a spirit of love (note the two aspects of worship: rising up to God's majesty and acknowledging our nothingness), the more we can be filled with mercy for all our neighbors, for all who lack what they need, in every order of perfection.

We can even say that it is through the close union between filial adoration and mercy that the sacrifice of Christ is, above all and before all, the royal sacrifice of love. The holocaust of Jesus on the Cross, reaching its completion with the wound in His heart, is truly the filial sacrifice of love, the gift of His whole earthly life, to save mankind and glorify the Father.

"He gave himself up for us, a fragrant offering and sacrifice to God" (Eph. 5:2). He gave Himself up in the freedom of love. He gave Himself up to God for us as an oblation and a victim; a sacrifice of pleasing fragrance. It is in truth He who worships, who offers Himself in sacrifice, who is given up for us. And this sacrifice is acceptable to God, for it is a sacrifice of love that is carried out through obedience. The freedom of love with which Jesus offers Himself is the inner freedom of the well-beloved children of the Father—a freedom that is not opposed to obedience, but

is carried out to the full only through perfect submission to
the Father's will. The more we are united to the Father's will,
the freer we are, since we are then joined to our true end. It
may be said, then, that the faithful, loving adoration of
Christ crucified is carried out through obedience, and this
obedience allows for this freedom in mercy and this abundant plenitude of merciful gift.

The sacrifice of the Cross, together with the mystery of
the Resurrection, is the visible witness to the omnipotence of
God's infinite love for Christ and His members. The sacrifice
of Elijah in the presence of the priests of Baal only prefigured
it. The true fire from Heaven is nothing else than the love of
the Father, which took possession of the soul and the will of
Jesus, in order to let Him divinely perform His actions, to make
a filial, loving act of adoration, the fruit of a moral virtue
wholly transfigured by divine love and exercised divinely under
the breath of Love, of the Spirit.

If we wish to understand the divine unity in the sacrifice of Christ crucified, the unity of the mystery of filial adoration and mercy, we must always return to this profound
action of the breath of Love who "renews the face of the
earth," who renews the image of God in the soul of Jesus and
in His mind and will.

The breath of Love, who dwells in the soul of Jesus,
transforms all His actions, both religious and merciful, uniting them in love. Again, the breath of Love, in the gift of
piety which interiorizes worship, turns the adoration of the
"servant" into a filial, loving adoration. God, as Father, is
then worshiped for His grandeur and majesty—as the One
who communicates life in all its fullness. That is the reason

this filial worship is at first carried out in the depths of Jesus' soul, in silence and in an utterly hidden and secret fashion. By means of the gift of piety, love introduces into the soul its own ways: its silence and its profound and secret way of acting. Love allows us to understand clearly that everything is related to the one supreme Love and that all which is not this substantial love of God is but "nothing."

The soul of Christ considers itself not only as "nothing," but also as at the service of all, judging itself as truly responsible for all sinners and all sins against the Father. In this lies the mystery of sadness that filled Jesus' soul and left it in such terrible isolation, abandoned by all. Through this weight of sadness and isolation, the annihilation in Jesus' soul was able to go so far, even into desolation, contempt, and rejection. The filial adoration in Jesus' soul could then experience an abyss of poverty and nothingness. One must "lose one's soul" in order to save it. That is indeed the mystery of His becoming an outcast and experiencing this to the full.

In the filial adoration of the Agony and of the Cross, we must contemplate the divine annihilation of Jesus' soul. Jesus willed and accepted this annihilation. It was accomplished through His human will being totally broken—"Not my will but thine"—to leave all to the loving will of the Father. This annihilation in love is joyful and peaceful but also violent and terrible; it crushes and breaks the soul of Jesus because the most noble, profound, and delicate bonds of the human heart must be broken and offered to His God, His Father. Jesus must not only accept separation from His Mother, John, and the disciples in the particular circumstances of the Cross, but He must also wound the hearts of

His Mother and His well-beloved disciple. This violent "annihilation" of the will makes the heart of Jesus a victim of love.

First of all an inward act, Love desires all. The breath of Love, by and through the gift of piety, makes adoration an inward act; yet, this very breath also causes the act of adoration to extend its influence over all the activities of the body and the heart of Jesus. Christ's whole human nature is affected by the breath of Love; all is offered as a holocaust of love; nothing is spared. Divine love is jealous and desires all without exception. Love cannot be contented with signs; it wants the reality. The holocaust of animals ordered by the Law had only the value of a sign and therefore was not enough: "Sacrifices and offerings thou hast not desired, but a body hast thou prepared for me" (Heb. 10:5). A reality that expresses the inner adoration is thus necessary. The body of Christ and His heart, as the blood-stained victim on the Cross, expresses most fully this worship of reparation and satisfaction. The "annihilation" and interior love, all that is alive in Jesus, must be consumed by the "heavenly fire."

On Calvary, the body of Christ Himself is temple, altar, and victim at the same time in the new liturgy. He is the Lamb and the scapegoat. He is the first-fruits of the world. Nothing can be more beautiful or more noble or precious than this holy tabernacle, this dwelling of God. All the riches and splendor of the Temple are nothing in comparison with the worth and divine beauty of the body and blood of Jesus. His body is the most beautiful among the children of men, and it is also the body of the well-beloved Son of the Father who "reflects the glory of God" (Heb. 1:3).

But the beauty of the body of Jesus is veiled during the great hour of Calvary. Only His weakness and vulnerability are exposed before all; and, even more deeply, His solidarity with all the dreadful consequences of sin is clearly apparent. The scapegoat hides the Lamb without blemish.

The breath of Love, by and through the gift of piety, transforms the exercise of the virtue of mercy in the heart of Jesus crucified. The divine practice of mercy is not content with relieving, helping, consoling, or paying with one's own person. Mercy wants to do more. The place of the sufferer must be taken: a substitution must be made, demanding a total gift of self. Jesus crucified gives all that He is. He gives His body as food and His blood as drink—a rich grazing land indeed.

St. Augustine understood this well when He said of Jesus crucified:

> He ate with us that which fills the storeroom of our misery; He drank the vinegar mixed with gall. That is what He found in our storeroom. But at the same time He invited us to His splendid banquet, to the heavenly feast, to the table of angels, where He Himself is the bread. Coming down on this earth He found every punishment in our storeroom, and He has not refused to sit at our table to feast on them, while, in return, He has promised us His own table (Sermon, 231, 5).

Divine mercy truly demands the gift of ourselves to our unhappy neighbor, who can do nothing for us in return. We must give all we have without thought of reward, an utterly free and absolutely unconditional gift. We must be willing to give even to those who will not make use of our gift or who will use it to a bad purpose. The mystery of the Eucharist shows us this gratuitous, unconditional, universal mercy. Jesus gives Himself to each person as though each was the only one to receive Him, as though each was the only sheep for whom, if necessary, the others would be abandoned; and yet He gives Himself to all without exception. The mystery of the Eucharist helps us understand the mystery of the mercy of the Cross.

This divine mercy also grants forgiveness without limit and especially requires us to come to the defense of those who have harmed us. Jesus on the Cross pleaded with the Father for those who insulted and crucified Him: "Father, forgive them; for they know not what they do" (Lk. 23:34).

This gift and this forgiveness, which are fully accomplished because of the demands proper to divine love, allow us to understand how mercy, when practiced in a divine way, far from contradicting filial adoration, presupposes and requires it. We can forgive those who have harmed us only if our heart is utterly seized by the love of a friend. Thanks to this real love that takes complete hold of us, the injury no longer affects us—we are totally focused on the one we love. This is true even from the human standpoint but can only be carried out fully thanks to the love of God and, above all, thanks to filial adoration, which hides us and encompasses us in the loving majesty of the Father.

Out of love for the Father, we are glad to forgive, to witness with our own eyes that His love alone matters for us, that His love is greater than these petty wounds.

The gift of self can equally be carried out only if we no longer belong to ourselves but belong to God. So long as we still belong to ourselves, we cannot offer ourselves with the total gratuity of mercy. Our deep egoism prevents it. If we love God, if we render to Him the worship of a son, we no longer belong to ourselves but belong wholly to Him and are wholly hidden in Him. It is He who disposes of us according to His good pleasure. For this reason, filial adoration is necessary for the full bestowal of mercy as gift and mercy as forgiveness. He who no longer lives this filial adoration cannot go as far in the practice of mercy.

The annihilation of filial adoration allows this fullness of gift and joy in forgiving. The mystery of the Cross is a wonderful proof, and here perhaps we see the most divine and most human aspect of the Cross. The "Good Shepherd" cannot be separated from the "Lamb of God."

We can understand how the sacrifice of the Cross, uniting in itself in an eminent way all the perfections of the Old Testament sacrifices, is truly, in its most essential nature, a sacrifice of love. It is truly the sacrifice of the new Law, which is the law of love. It is just for this reason that this sacrifice, an act of filial and loving worship, leads directly to a new revelation of God's mystery.

If we can start with the truth that every sacrifice of the Old Testament is a revelation to us of God's mystery, this applies still more truly to the sacrifice of Christ. For the Old Testament sacrifices give only rough images of the truth. They are stages in the revelation of the mysteries of God, who is formally distinct from these sacrifices, while the sacrifice of Christ lies at the end of Christ's apostolic life, at the end of

His personal revelation, as a summary and completion of His whole apostolic life and teaching. On the Cross, Christ gives us His testament of love, and we must look for His final teaching in the mystery of the Cross.

Our final understanding, therefore, of the mystery of God and His attributes must be found in the mystery of Christ crucified. Hence, after trying to make clear the essential nature of this sacrifice, the ending of His life, we should try to grasp the way in which it unveils to us, in an ultimate manner, the whole greatness of God's mystery: His love, His simplicity, His mercy, His justice, His omnipotence and His intimacy, His jealousy and His light, His charity and His holiness.

CHAPTER 3

CHRIST CRUCIFIED, OUR WISDOM: THE REVELATION OF GOD'S MYSTERY

THE SACRIFICE OF THE CROSS:
THE REVELATION OF THE MYSTERY OF
THE LOVE AND SIMPLICITY OF THE FATHER

W HEN Pilate asked Jesus about His mission, He replied: " 'For this I was born, and for this I have come into the world, to bear witness to the truth.' Pilate said to Him, 'What is truth?' " (Jn. 18:37-38). Jesus did not answer Pilate.

For our part, we know that "God is Love," that all truth depends on this unique truth which is the truth. Hence, all the Law and the prophets are summed up in this one commandment of love. If God is Love, the Law must lead to love, and it follows still more plainly that the prophets must themselves lead to love.

The whole earthly life of Christ was aimed at giving this testimony: "For this I was born, to bear witness to the truth." It is by living to the fullest extent this mystery of divine love, as the beloved Son of the Father, that Jesus bears witness to the truth. All His actions teach us that we should love God, that we should understand His love, that we should love Him as a well-loved Father. Jesus is the beloved Son in whom the Father is well pleased, and He alone can reveal to us the mystery of the love of His beloved Father. From the crib, as a small, weak, silent child, He reveals to us this mystery of the simplicity and love of the beloved Father. The first explicit teaching mentioned in the Gospel tells us that He is wholly engaged in the affairs of His Father. Throughout His apostolic life He leads us to the Father and lets us gradually discover His love, but it is above all on the Cross that He shows us, in the sacrifice offered for the glory of the Father and the salvation of His sheep, the infinite mystery of God's love. For this reason, the Cross is, above and beyond all, a work of filial love and can be the most profound revelation of love.

Love is not expressed, or certainly is always ill expressed, in words; it can be expressed only by love and through love. Now, the mysteries of the Agony, of the Crucifixion, and of the Burial are precisely and above all mysteries of the filial love of Jesus for His Father. Hence, only these mysteries can reveal, through a certain connaturality, the secret of God's mystery, namely, His love. These mysteries are openings that let us catch sight of the infinite love of the Father. It is through these mysteries that our Lord gives us His ultimate teaching. These mysteries (the Agony, Crucifixion, and Burial) considered simply in the light of justice, and even of the virtue of religion, remain incomprehensible. From the sole point of view of justice, we cannot understand why such an extreme experience of sadness, pain, and humiliation should have been permitted, when a single act of humility on the part of Jesus, having infinite value, could have made full satisfaction for all the sins of the world. From the point of view of the virtue of religion alone, the offering of the first-fruits of the earth by the Incarnate Word would by itself have had infinite value, declaring the sovereign rights of the Creator of the universe.

If we consider these mysteries as completing the great evangelical revelation of the love of God, as the testament of the new covenant, which is a covenant of love, then everything regains its full meaning. Nothing is out of place when it serves to glorify the love of the Father by declaring His exclusive rights as well-loved Father, when it serves to manifest the infinite greatness of God's love. Christ crucified has indeed become, by the power of God, our wisdom, our wisdom of love. It is foolishness to our little human reason—it was unnecessary to go to such lengths—a scandal to our human feelings. Being able to give in Jesus crucified a supreme witness to the mystery of God's love, Wisdom has done everything to give this witness: death itself has contributed to this great epiphany of the mystery of God as Love.

If the whole of the Old Testament, from the standpoint of knowledge of God, is dominated by the revelation made to Moses on Mount Horeb when God revealed His name: "I AM WHO AM"—Yahweh (Ex. 3:14)—the revelation of Christ crucified completes and perfects this revelation. Our Lord Himself tells us plainly: "When you have lifted up the Son of man, then you will know that I am" (Jn. 8:28).

The "I am" of Jesus crucified is that of the Son declaring that "God is love" (1 Jn. 4:8, 16) and bearing witness to

His love. In the silence of sadness and suffering, He expresses all God's love. By means of this new burning bush and in the flame of fire, the mystery of the Father's goodness is indeed revealed. We must try to understand the greatness of these two revelations, which put us in the presence of God and His mystery.

When God revealed to Moses that He is the Lord: "I AM WHO AM," He did not do so spontaneously. It was Moses who wished to know His name in order to present himself to Pharaoh with more authority. Before this, God had spontaneously declared Himself in a far simpler way: "I am the God of your father, the God of Abraham, the God of Isaac, and the God of Jacob" (Ex. 3:6).

To this exile (and doubly exiled), God declared Himself as the God of his tribe, of his fathers, as one in whom he could trust fully, for He had made a covenant with Abraham, and the covenant continued to apply to all of his race. Moses could then rely on this covenant. By declaring Himself in this way, God declared Himself as the one true God, as the God from on high, whom Jacob loved and worshiped and to whom Abraham had been faithful. Moses, therefore, at once "hid his face, for he was afraid to look at God" (Ex. 3:6).

By this act of making Himself nothing, by this act of adoration, he showed that he, too, believed that the God of his fathers was the one God.

When Moses asked Him His name, it was to reassure himself and gain courage to confront Pharaoh, to bind himself to Him in a more personal way, and to be able to use the authority of God Himself. When a man introduces himself in the name of someone else, he is clothed with his authority and shares in his power. In calling Himself the Lord: "I am the God who is," God unveiled the mystery of His absolute transcendence. This was necessary; He had to reveal Himself as having authority over Pharaoh, for otherwise it would have been no help to Moses.

When God revealed Himself as the God of Abraham and Isaac and Jacob, Moses' heart was directly touched, for Moses believed in the promise, in the covenant made with his fathers. This revelation continued to concern only the people of Israel. To Pharaoh, the God of Israel was the God of a people who were in exile, oppressed and enslaved; He was the God of the ones he was trying to oppress. Moses could not present himself to Pharaoh clothed with the authority of the God of his fathers. He knew what Pharaoh would think of this, having been brought up in his vicinity.

Revealing Himself as "the God who is," the Lord, God revealed Himself as He who is first, He on whom all depends, He who has the right to give orders to Pharaoh. That the meaning of the revelation might be better understood, it was in fact accompanied by the grant to Moses of the power to change his staff into a serpent and then the serpent back into a staff. It became a rod in his hand—"that they may believe that the Lord, the God of their fathers, the God of Abraham, the God of Isaac, and the God of Jacob, has appeared to you" (Ex. 4:4-5).

Revealing Himself as the "God who is," God revealed His name, that which expresses what He is, His own person. The name of a person expresses what is most personal to him, what best characterizes him, and what distinguishes him most plainly from other persons and other realities. To be told someone's name is to be able to call upon him when we wish. It is to be able to attract his attention and converse with him. Thus, it is to possess a certain claim upon him. God tells His name to Moses precisely in order to give Him confidence and show him that He will not abandon him, that he can go forward and "Yahweh" will always be with him. The name that expresses this mystery of God, that tells us what is unique in God, is an ineffable name—Yahweh—a name that cannot be named, meaning "He is." This is how God declares Himself to Moses, when he asks His name: "I AM WHO AM."

God uses the verb "to be" to express what He is. He uses the verb which has the most common and general meaning. Certainly the verb "to be" is present in all our assertions, whether implicitly or explicitly. It has also the most basic and profound meaning, for, if a reality is not, we can make no assertion about it. Since it has the deepest significance of all, no one else can claim for a name "I am who is," that is, "I am he who is before all, at the source of all." Hence, in calling Himself the Lord, God both hides and reveals Himself.[14] He makes clear to Moses that He cannot be defined, for a definition cannot be given by using a verb that is the basis of all our assertions. To give Himself such a name is to disavow any particular characteristic and so any kind of definition. God cannot be defined, for, in order to

---

14. Cf. Bible de Jerusalem, ed. du Cerf, 1956, p. 63—with reference to the two interpretations of the name of the Lord—one emphasizing the negative aspect: God avoids the question and declares, "I am who I am," the other, emphasizing the positive aspect: "I am He who is." In general, tradition has preferred the second of the two.

define God, we should have to reach something beyond being.

Calling Himself Yahweh, He also reveals Himself in a wonderful way. He reveals the absolute simplicity of His being since He has no other determination, no other characteristic, but to be. In giving Himself the name, "I am," He reveals to us that He is before all that exists in a particular manner. He Himself exists in an absolute manner, while all other realities exist only in a partial, particular manner.

Thus, He also contrasts Himself with other gods, who are but nothing. He contrasts Himself with the gods of Pharaoh, who are nothing and can do nothing. Even though Pharaoh does not acknowledge the Lord as the one true God, this does not affect the fact that "He is." The initial seed of this revelation made to Moses will become more explicit in the prophets and acquire an extraordinary strength. Here I will only quote some passages from the prophet Isaiah:

> I am the Lord, that is my name; my glory I give to no other, nor my praise to graven images (42:8).

> Before me no god was formed, nor shall there be any after me. I, I am the Lord, and besides me there is no savior. . . . I am God, and also henceforth I am He; there is none who can deliver from my hand; I work and who can hinder it (43:10-11, 13)?

> I am the first and I am the last; besides me there is no god. Who is like me (44:6-7)?

> I am the Lord, and there is no other, besides
> me there is no God; I gird you, though you do
> not know me, that men may know, from the
> rising of the sun and from the west, that there
> is none besides me (45:5-6; cf. 46:5-7; 48:11).

> I am the Lord, and there is no other. I form
> light and create darkness, I make weal and
> create woe, I am the Lord, who do all these
> things (45:6-7).

> Truly, thou art a God who hidest thyself, O
> God of Israel, the Savior. All of them are put
> to shame and confounded, the makers of idols
> go in confusion together (45:15-16).

Revealing Himself as "Yahweh"—"I am the God who
is"—He reveals Himself as the Master of all because He is
before all and all things depend on Him. For that reason, He
has no rival, for nothing is equal to Him. He is not relative to
anything, but all is relative to Him, and so His name can
only be "the God who is." No other name can be so simple
or better express the absolute simplicity of the source of
all or better express the transcendence of the Creator of the
universe.

The revelation on Mount Horeb is still true. He who
gave us His name that we might be able to call upon Him is
still the same Lord. It is our part to receive this revelation
with faith and live in accordance with it. On the Cross, however, the Lord revealed Himself to us in a new way: "I am"
is "the Savior" who gives Himself to us through love. Jesus'

sacrifice on the Cross is the new burning bush, which reveals that God, in all His being, in all the purity and simplicity of His being, is love. If God were not love in all His being, in all that He is, the sacrifice of Jesus on the Cross, of Him who said "I am," could have no meaning; it would be foolishness and a scandal. If God is Love, this sacrifice is indeed "wisdom," the great manifestation of love.

The new "sign," given to us that we may understand that God is Love in all His being, that "I am" is love, is the Resurrection of Jesus' body, the Resurrection of the Lamb, the glorification of His wounded heart—the wood of life becomes a serpent (loaded with all the iniquity of the world, He is the cursed and abandoned one), and the serpent, the cursed one, becomes again the wood of life.

The "hand of God," on the Cross and during the Agony, is covered with leprosy, white as snow, being plunged in the Father's will, but it reappears as totally clean, being hidden in the will of the Father and in His love.[15]

Jesus' bloody sacrifice reveals to us above all how absolute is the love of God. God is Love; His love is as simple as His being. In us, love is always relative and divided. It is not first. We cannot be love in all our being. There is in the depths of our being a certain metaphysical egoism, which limits our love at the root. We can love only in successive acts

---

15. This is the second sign given to Moses: " 'Put your hand into your bosom.' And he put his hand into his bosom; and when he took it out, behold, his hand was leprous, as white as snow. Then God said, 'Put your hand back into your bosom.' So he put his hand back into his bosom; and when he took it out, behold, it was restored like the rest of his flesh" (Ex. 4:6-7).

that always remain, whatever their intensity and vehemence, accidental, that is, always an addition to our substantial being. This gap in every creature between its substantial being and its love, whether passional or spiritual, shows how radically limited are our hearts, which cannot set on fire our whole being. When our heart does seem to consume our being, this is only a passing impression; in reality, it is not all on fire. There is always something which cannot burn, which cannot change into fire, that is, into love. On the other hand, all God's Being is "Love," for He is love. Even the Old Testament declared the love of God.

The use of the symbol of fire to express the active presence of God is very clear (cf. Gen. 15:17: the covenant with Abraham; Ex. 13:21: the pillar of fire, leading Israel across the desert; Ex. 19:18: Sinai on fire). The very name of the Lord was revealed to Moses from the burning bush. The angel of the Lord manifested himself to Moses under the form of a flame of fire bursting from a bush: "the bush was burning, yet it was not consumed" (Ex. 3:2); "And Mount Sinai was wrapped in smoke, because the Lord descended upon it in fire" (Ex. 19:18); on Mount Carmel, we are told: "the fire of the Lord fell, and consumed the burnt offering, and the wood" (1 Kings 18:38).

Apart from the symbolism of fire, we are told expressly that God loved His people, and hence, that He is love. It is especially with the prophets that we find the deeper revelations of the Lord's heart:

> "The people who survived the sword found
> grace in the wilderness; when Israel sought for

rest, the Lord appeared to him from afar. I have loved you with an everlasting love; therefore I have continued my faithfulness to you" (Jer. 31:2-3, cf. Deut. 4:37; 10:15; Is. 43:4). "Be mindful of thy mercy, O Lord, and of thy steadfast love" (Ps. 25:6).

In the prophet Hosea the revelation of God's love is still clearer:

"When Israel was a child, I loved him, and out of Egypt I called my son. The more I called them, the more they went from me. . . . Yet it was I who taught Ephraim to walk, I took them up in my arms; but they did not know that I healed them. I led them with cords of compassion, with the bands of love, and I became to them as one who eases the yoke on their jaws, and I bent down to them and fed them" (Hos. 11:1-4).

After the exile, the Lord again declared His love for Israel:

Fear not, for you will not be ashamed; be not confounded, for you will not be put to shame; for you will forget the shame of your youth, and the reproach of your widowhood you will remember no more. For your Maker is your husband, the Lord of hosts is his name; and the Holy One of Israel is your Redeemer, the

God of the whole earth he is called. For the
Lord has called you like a wife forsaken and
grieved in spirit, like a wife of youth when
she is cast off, says your God. For a brief
moment I forsook you, but with great compassion I will gather you. In overflowing
wrath for a moment I hid my face from you,
but with everlasting love I will have compassion on you, says the Lord, your Redeemer
(Is. 54:4-8).[16]

To show the quality of this love the Lord says with great
emphasis: ". . . for you shall worship no other god, for the
Lord, whose name is Jealous, is a jealous God" (Ex. 34:14).
He stands no partition in this love.

The mystery of the Incarnation manifests the mystery of
the love of God to us. Love is brought about through personal gift. By giving us His Son, and by giving Him in the
way in which He has chosen to give Him, God makes us
understand how much He loves us; and thus we discover the
sweetness and power of His love: "In this the love of God was
made manifest among us, that God sent his only Son into the
world, so that we might live through him. In this is love, not
that we loved God but that he loved us and sent his Son to
be the expiation for our sins" (1 Jn. 4:9-10; cf. Jn. 3:16).

The sacrifice of the Cross reveals to us with fresh force
the "jealousy" of His love, its absolute quality, and, at a still

---

16. We should also remember the Song of Solomon, which expresses
clearly the power and primacy of love.

deeper level, how much His love is primary and substantial. The death of Christ, freely accepted, which witnesses to the love of the Father, is stronger than death; it is victorious over every death. Death alone can be a sign of the absolute and substantial primacy of God's love.

Every word and every human action other than death can be corrected, repaired, completed, and perfected, for all these actions are essentially relative, while death alone affects us in a way that is total and definitive; it cannot be corrected or perfected. Death alone is without remedy, for it is a substantial separation. It alone in our physical world imposes itself in an absolute fashion. It is the only visible and almost palpable absolute within our reach; thus, it is both terrible and fascinating. Our sensibilities tremble at it, for they do not love it but sense it to be an enemy. Our sensibilities are at ease only with relativity and movement; but our intelligence, in its purest, most spiritual, and most immaterial element, is drawn toward death, so to speak, or, to be more accurate, can be seduced by it on account of the thirst of the intelligence both for experience and principles. Now, death presents itself to us both as an original and still untried experience and as a principle—it is true that this principle is a negative one, yet it is a principle nonetheless, for it is an absolute ending.

We see then that, due to its sensible character and its quality of being an absolute, an end-point, death can be used by God's wisdom as the sign that is best able to express clearly the greatness of His love: which is substantial, eternal, and incomparable.

In this life, when man loves, he already judges—with his modest wisdom of love—that only death can express the intensity of his love. Do not lovers claim that their love is stronger than death? If they could, would they not make use of death to prove their love?

What human love stirs up only as an abstract desire (since human love depends on the present condition of being alive and would destroy itself by death), God's love can truly accomplish. Such love is in truth stronger than death; it rules over death and can make use of it to proclaim its own absolute character and supremacy.

Christ's death on the Cross, freely accepted through love, witnesses plainly to the supremacy of God's love, the love of the Father.

Since divine Wisdom makes use of the death of the Man-God on Calvary to manifest the substantial character of God's love, it is fitting that Wisdom should make use of it to the full. Hence it is that all the deaths man can suffer are, as it were, gathered together in this one death. In the death of Christ, all deaths possess an extreme and incredible intensity, in their various degrees, in order to assert all the more emphatically that God's love alone is substantial Love, pure Love.

Let us think of the unperceived and solitary death of the Agony in the Garden—"My soul is very sorrowful, even to death" (Mk. 14:34). Agony and terror shatter and oppress Him. This was the deep inner death of the soul, which today we would call the death of our psychological Ego, of our psychological personality. Jesus utterly gives up His whole human will before the will of the Father: "not what I will, but what thou wilt." This was a hidden and infinitely mysterious death, in which Jesus effaces Himself and is willing to be, as it were, forsaken: death in sadness, anguish, and strife.

Then comes the kiss of Judas, the sign of betrayal; the cowardice of the disciples who, seeing Jesus seized, flee away; the denial of Peter, in whom Jesus had placed such trust. Betrayal, cowardice, denial: these are truly the different ways the heart of a friend can die. Betrayal of a friend is indeed death to friendship in the strictest sense; and here death is accompanied by cowardice and denial, that it may be complete in its intensity and consequences. Only one remains faithful. This is truly a profound death for the human heart, if we realize that friendship is one of the deepest ways in which the human heart can flourish.

All the humiliations of the Praetorium, when He was scorned and derided by the soldiers who thought Him a vain madman, when the Chief Priests regarded Him as a blasphemer who did not respect God's rights, when He was considered a dangerous adventurer who might seduce the people, when the life of the criminal Barabbas was chosen before His life, and when He was condemned to the most degrading of punishments, the punishment of slaves—He experienced every humiliation, and through these humiliations He experienced every degradation, political and religious. He died to the life of a free citizen, a member of a political society. He died to the life of a religious man, a member of a religious society. These are truly deaths, for there is a real human development on both these levels.

Then, the Crucifixion meant physical death, the violent and bloody death of the Cross, led up to by the Scourging and Crowning with thorns, that this death might be still more cruel and shameful. This form of death is the most painful and violent possible.

Even His corpse was not respected: "When they came to Jesus and saw that he was already dead, they did not break his legs. But one of the soldiers pierced his side with a spear" (Jn. 19:33-34). It was necessary that His breast be opened and His heart pierced so that the last drop of His blood might be shed. This final death of His corpse was necessary; Jesus, being dead, could speak no longer, but His heart could still bleed.

Each of these deaths, together with the different corresponding manners of His Resurrection, bear witness that the love of God is the only eternal, substantial love. It is the only faithful love, the only love that is the source of life. And all these deaths culminate in the wounding of Jesus' heart. This open wound in the heart of Jesus is, as it were, a divine opening that lays bare the abyss of God's love, which gives it to us and reveals it, which expresses it as a reality for us.

Through His wounded side, through His martyr's heart, we can enter as by a royal door, narrow indeed, in order to contemplate the mystery of the filial love by which the Son is wholly delivered to the gracious will of the Father, who truly loves His beloved Son. "For this reason the Father loves me, because I lay down my life, that I may take it again. No one takes it from me, but I lay it down of my own accord. I have power to lay it down, and I have power to take it again; this charge I have received from my Father. . . . And he who sent me is with me; he has not left me alone, for I always do what is pleasing to him" (Jn. 10:17-18; 8:29).

In the love of the Son is revealed to us the love of the Father for the beloved Son, the mystery of the love of God, as it had never yet been revealed. It is truly the jealous God

and His exclusive, substantial, intimate love that is revealed
and given to us.

When we touch upon the love of God, we touch upon
what is deepest, most interior, most personal in God, so to
speak. It is indeed, as it were, the "heart" of God which is
revealed to us in the heart of Jesus crucified, in and through
the wounded heart of Christ. This revelation is so that we may
understand that, while no creature can touch God in the simplicity of His being (since He is one whom we cannot affect
but who rather acts on us), God, in the fullness of His love,
is the most vulnerable of beings—the being in whom there is
no hardness, or egoism, or bitter, cold, indifferent turning in
upon Himself, for God is Love. It is truly love which makes
us attentive and receptive to others, love which makes us able
to experience the feelings of others, to live what they live.
God, in His all that He is, is love. Hence, in all that He is,
He is receptivity. He is one who draws us to Himself and
wishes to hide us in the very mystery of His love.

While the covenant of the first Passover was made in the
light and the mystery of the simplicity of Him who said: "I
am the God who is," the covenant of the true, ultimate
Passover, which frees us from the slavery of sin, is made in the
light of the mystery of love. It is made in the light of Him
who gives to us in silence the wounded heart of His beloved
Son as a sign of supreme love.

We should understand that this revelation of God's love,
far from contradicting the revelation of His simplicity of
being, gives it, on the contrary, its profound meaning; for in
God simplicity of being and love are but one. The love of
God is simple and pure; God is the very purity of love. The

simplicity of God's being is love. It is no mere abstract simplicity or a simplicity of poverty or naiveté. It is the simplicity of one who is perfect in love, with a clear, burning
simplicity. It is the very simplicity of love. Scripture makes
use of the symbol of a dove to help us understand this simplicity of love and to express its freshness and richness. God
always loves as though in a first act of love, and He always
loves as though it were the ultimate act of love.

Horeb and the Cross are indeed inseparable; the two
Passovers are inseparable.

THE SACRIFICE OF THE CROSS:
THE REVELATION OF THE MYSTERY OF
THE JUSTICE AND MERCY OF THE FATHER

The sacrifice of the Cross reveals to us the mystery of the
substantial love of God, but it also reveals to us His mercy and
justice in a new way. It reveals to us especially the close harmony in God between these two divine attributes, which
have already been revealed so emphatically in the Old Testament and which may sometimes appear contradictory.

First, we shall see how the sacrifice of the Cross gives the
revelation of justice and mercy and then how, by giving this
revelation, it leads up to their divine harmony.

The revelation of God's justice begins right from the
first pages of Scripture. After the sin of Adam and Eve, we see
how God judges Adam and Eve and the serpent, conferring
on each a punishment in proportion to the sin (Gen. 3:14-
19). There is an act of judging and an act of justice, for God
is both the person offended, as law-giver, and the judge. So,
too, with Cain, when he killed Abel, we see God judging by

punishing the slayer of his brother (Gen. 4:10-16). Again, the flood is an act of justice on the part of the Lord (Gen. 5:7) as also is the scattering of those who wished to build the tower of Babel (Gen. 11:8). At the end of revelation, in the Apocalypse, the justice of God still appears to have great importance in God's government.[17]

Throughout the whole of Scripture, this mystery of God's justice is stated clearly. At the same time, however, something still more mysterious has been revealed to us: certain acts of forgiveness, protection, care, and pity; the just God is also merciful. Before the sin of Adam, when God says: "It is not good that the man should be alone" (Gen. 2:18), God's gratuitous solicitude and concern for Adam is revealed. In the cases of Abel and Noah, the merciful goodness of God is revealed: "And the Lord had regard for Abel and His offering" (Gen. 4:4). "Noah found favor in the eyes of the Lord"; this is especially evident in the covenant that the Lord made with Noah: "I will never again curse the ground because of man, for the imagination of man's heart is evil from his youth" (Gen. 8:21).

But it is especially in regard to the patriarchs, and perhaps still more in regard to Moses, that the mercy of the Lord is manifested fully. Appearing to Moses, He says: "I have seen the affliction of my people who are in Egypt, and have heard their cry because of their taskmasters; I know their sufferings, and I have come down to deliver them out of the hand of the Egyptians, and to bring them up out of that land to a good and broad land, a land flowing with milk and honey" (Ex. 3:7-8).

---

17. Cf. Rev. 15:5; 18:1-3; 19:11-16.

This is a wonderful description of the merciful God; He has seen the misery of His people. The first requirement of mercy is to know the unhappiness of the other person. It is necessary to be very attentive to find out the misery and to be able to look at it squarely. Yet it must be looked at with the gaze of a friend; otherwise it will cause fear. To look at misery merely for the sake of looking at it, to use it as an experiment, is surely inhuman. What would we think of a doctor who undid a patient's dressing, thereby causing him pain, merely to see and observe the state of the wound? God has seen the misery of His people.

The second requirement of mercy is to be compassionate to the other person's misery, to know it as though it were our own. Everything must be done to comfort the unhappy: "I have come down to deliver them out of the hand of the Egyptians." God wished to make use of Moses in order to carry out this great act of mercy toward His people. And this is the way in which God showed His mercy: He wished to do so with special delicacy, to save His people by means of a member of His people. This was part of God's merciful ways, for God did not need Moses in order to carry out His will; but He wished to make use of him, in order that His act of mercy might be the more perfect and fitting for the unhappy people He wished to deliver. In front of the objections and hesitations of Moses, who was afraid to carry out such a mission, the Lord revealed Himself as full of goodness toward him—He promised to be with him and to help him to speak.

By mercifully delivering His people, the Lord punished Pharaoh. Within this very act of such wonderful mercy toward

the people of Israel, an ever sterner justice is shown to Pharaoh. This justice appears in full force during the Passover,
with its destroying angel, and during the passage across the
Red Sea (Ex. 11:4; 12:29; 14:15 ff.).

The wanderings of the people of Israel in the desert
under God's guidance is repeatedly punctuated by acts of mercy
of the Lord, who is watching over His people, but it is also
punctuated by a series of punishments and acts of divine
justice, calling Israel back to the right path whenever the
people grumble and wish to turn back (Ex. 15:23). These
wanderings under God's guidance make a wonderful spiritual journey, showing us how God, in His wisdom, mar-
velously doses out His merciful treatment, His trials or His
punishments.

This is shown very clearly in the first stage, when they
came to Marah. After three days in the desert without finding any water, an oasis was reached, but its water was too bitter to drink. Here is the trial. The people grumbled, and
God, having compassion on them, used Moses to change the
bitter water into sweet water; and He declared: "I am the
Lord, your healer" (Ex. 15:26). The Lord, however, made it
plain that He would not show this mercy unless the people
did what was right in His sight and unless they listened to
His commandments and obeyed His laws.

This duality is also very apparent with the Ten Commandments given to Moses on Mount Sinai. It was an act of
mercy to wish to re-educate the people of Israel and give
them a sense of religion once again, teaching them how to
worship; but to re-educate them by giving them the Law was
a striking act of justice.

Moses acknowledges this in His great canticle: "the Rock, his work is perfect; for all his ways are justice" (Deut. 32:4). The precise purpose of justice is to render to each man His due. Justice considers what is right. Moses adds: "God of faithfulness and without iniquity, just and right is he" (Deut. 32:4). But He is also merciful, and so Moses can declare:

> He found him in a desert land, and in the howling waste of wilderness; he encircled him, he cared for him, he kept him as the apple of his eye. Like an eagle that stirs up its nest, that flutters over its young, spreading out its wings, catching them, bearing them on its pinions, the Lord alone did lead him, and there was no foreign god with him. He made them ride on the high places of the earth, and he ate the produce of the field (Deut. 32:10-13).

The prophets never cease proclaiming, recalling, and singing of the mercy and justice that characterize the works of the Lord. Let us quote only the more important passages, which take us deeper into this mystery.

In her canticle of thanksgiving, Hannah acknowledges that the Lord is a God of justice and mercy:

> The Lord is a God of knowledge, and by him actions are weighed. The bows of the mighty are broken, but the feeble gird on strength. Those who are full have hired themselves out for bread, but those who were hungry have

ceased to hunger. The barren has borne seven, but she who has seven children is forlorn. The Lord kills and brings to life; he brings down to Sheol and raises up. The Lord makes poor and makes rich; he brings low, he also exalts. He raises up the poor from the dust; he lifts the needy from the ash heap, to make them sit with princes and inherit a seat of honor. . . . The Lord will judge the ends of the earth (1 Sam. 2:3-8, 10).

In Psalm 89, the glory and power of the Lord are praised, and we are told "righteousness and justice are the foundation of thy throne; steadfast love and faithfulness go before thee" (Ps. 89:14).[18]

In Psalms 9, 25 and 119, we find the theme developed at length:

But the Lord sits enthroned forever, he has established his throne for judgment; and he judges the world with righteousness, he judges the peoples with equity. The Lord is a stronghold for the oppressed, a stronghold in times of trouble. And those who know thy name put their trust in thee, for thou, O Lord, hast not forsaken those who seek thee. . . . Be

---

18. Cf. Ps. 19:9-10: "The ordinances of the Lord are true, and righteous altogether. More to be desired are they than gold, even much fine gold; sweeter also than honey and drippings of the honeycomb."

gracious to me, O Lord! Behold what I suffer from those who hate me. . . .[19] The Lord has made himself known, he has executed judgment; the wicked are snared in the work of their own hands. . . .[20] For the needy shall not always be forgotten, and the hope of the poor shall not perish for ever. . . . The hapless commits himself to thee; thou hast been the helper of the fatherless (Ps. 9:7-10, 13, 16, 18; 10:14).

Good and upright is the Lord; therefore he instructs sinners in the way. He leads the humble in what is right, and teaches the humble his way. . . . For thy name's sake, O Lord, pardon my guilt, for it is great. . . . Consider my affliction and my trouble, and forgive all my sins. . . . Oh, guard my life, and deliver me; let me not be put to shame, for I take refuge in thee. May integrity and uprightness preserve me, for I wait for thee (Ps. 25:8-9, 11, 18, 20-21).

Righteous art thou, O Lord, and right are thy judgments. . . . Thy righteousness is righteous for ever, and thy law is true. . . . Look on my

---

19. Cf. Ps. 25:16.

20. Cf. 2 Sam. 22:25: "Therefore the Lord has recompensed me according to my righteousness, according to my cleanness in his sight."

affliction and deliver me, for I do not forget
thy law (Ps. 119:137, 142, 153).

In Jeremiah, Hosea, and Ezekiel, the mercy of the Lord is
shown with special tenderness. Speaking of Jacob, the Lord says:

> For I will restore health to you, and your
> wounds I will heal. . . . Thus says the Lord:
> Behold, I will restore the fortunes of the tents
> of Jacob, and have compassion on his dwellings;
> the city shall be rebuilt upon its mound, and
> the palace shall stand where it used to be. Out
> of them shall come songs of thanksgiving, and
> the voices of those who make merry. I will
> multiply them, and they shall not be few; I
> will make them honored, and they shall not be
> small. . . . He who scattered Israel will gather
> him, and will keep him as a shepherd keeps his
> flock. For the Lord has ransomed Jacob, and has
> redeemed him from hands too strong for him.
> . . . I will turn their mourning into joy, I will
> comfort them, and give them gladness for sor-
> row (Jer. 30:17, 18-19; 31:10-11, 13).

> I will heal their faithlessness; I will love them
> freely, for my anger has turned from them. I
> will be as the dew to Israel; he shall blossom
> as the lily, he shall strike root as the poplar, his
> shoots shall spread out (Hos. 14:4-6).

> My heart recoils within me, my compassion
> grows warm and tender. I will not execute my

fierce anger, I will not again destroy Ephraim
(Hos. 11:8-9).

I myself will search for my sheep, and will seek
them out. . . . so will I seek out my sheep; and
I will rescue them from all places where they
have been scattered on a day of clouds and
thick darkness. . . . I will feed them with good
pasture, and upon the mountain heights of
Israel shall be their pasture; there they shall lie
down in good grazing land, and on fat pasture
they shall feed on the mountains of Israel. . . .
I will seek the lost, and I will bring back the
strayed, and I will bind up the crippled, and I
will strengthen the weak, and the fat and the
strong I will watch over; I will feed them in
justice (Ezek. 34:11-16).

Isaiah announces the glorious future of Israel:

For the Lord is our judge, the Lord is our ruler,
the Lord is our king; he will save us. . . . Then
prey and spoil in abundance will be divided;
even the lame will take the prey. And no inhab-
itant will say, "I am sick"; the people who
dwell there will be forgiven their iniquity. . .
. I, I am he that comforts you (Is. 33:22-24;
51:12).

The sacrifice of the Cross is supremely a work of the
"uprightness" of the Father and a work of His mercy; the two
are intimately connected. The sacrifice of the Cross is the

supreme work of justice. The justice of God was never as pure, as strict, as exact, as on the Cross. When this justice is employed toward the sinner, he is incapable of enduring the strict justice of God, for he is incapable of making amends for the offense against God and His love, which is a consequence of the sin he has freely committed in his pride and disobedience.

The justice of God could be employed perfectly toward Christ, the Man-God, who is infinitely pure but who, out of mercy, takes upon Himself all the sins of the world. In strict justice, Jesus can make amends for all the offenses of mankind because He is the Incarnate Word, and so He is God. All the deaths Jesus suffered during the Agony, on the Cross, in the Burial, He endured heroically, with an extraordinary intensity and awareness. All these deaths were punishments due to the sins of men, which He was willing to bear as if they were His own punishment, as if He, the just one, really deserved them. He bore them in order to satisfy God's justice, in order to pay the terrible debt of sinful humanity— of the unfaithful adulteress woman, to use the symbolism of Scripture.

By His willingness to satisfy every demand of justice in full, Jesus crucified shows us the greatness and gravity of God's justice, which is in no way arbitrary but is the wisdom of God. By this means, Jesus makes us understand more clearly the atrociousness of the sin that opposes and despises this justice. Jesus loves the Father's justice and His law. By being crucified, He became its defender. Not an "iota" of the Law must be lost, for it is written on stone by the finger of God. The Pharisees are false defenders of the Law and of

God's justice, for they defend it in its literal meaning, its
material application, without concerning themselves with the
spirit that gives it life or with the intentions of those who
obey it. To them, the essential thing is that the Law be
applied and that no external reproach be made to them. They
turn the Law into a kind of artistic standard for their lives.
Jesus respects the Law and defends it by living according to
its spirit, by making His intention conform to that of the
lawgiver. Hence, He truly fulfills it in His sacrifice on the
Cross.

For on the Cross the purpose of the Law is realized in an
eminent way: in Jesus crucified, the people of Israel worship
God in a unique manner. All the commandments are
supremely carried out in Jesus crucified. Hence, the Law is
fulfilled through the Crucifixion and has no further reason to
exist.[21]

The Resurrection of Christ's body, which occurred
secretly in the sepulcher, is the supreme work of justice of the
great Judge who gives to every man his due. To Christ crucified, to the Lamb who was slain, is due the glorification of
the Resurrection. To Christ crucified, who had experienced
poverty and humiliation to the full, is due in virtue of divine
justice the wonderful and everlasting exaltation on the night
of the Passover. To the wounded, humiliated heart of Christ
crucified is due that immense exaltation and glorification.
The risen heart of the Lamb is the source of all the light of
the heavenly Jerusalem.

---

21. What is true of the Cross is also true of all the other activities of
    Christ from the time of His conception.

This supreme work of the Father's "uprightness" allows us to reflect on this "uprightness" of God. God is just; He is justice. By saying this, we express an attribute of God, one of the qualities of His will and His being. We imply indeed that God gives to each one his due, while understanding that God owes nothing to any creature, but in creating them, gives them all that their being requires, that they may share as perfectly as possible in His goodness. To be just is, for God, to bring about that order which wisdom has willed in all things, an order expressed and proclaimed by the Law. The justice of the Father is manifested on the Cross precisely because Christ made reparation for sins and reestablished the order upset by disobedience. Christ fulfilled the Law by His obedience.

Again, justice is manifested by the Resurrection because it brings about what is due to Christ crucified. The sacrifice of the Cross is the supreme work of God's mercy, of a mercy that is exercised in a sweet and gentle manner. God wishes to save mankind, to forgive their sins by means of one among themselves, of Him who is "King" of mankind, and who, being both God and man, can make amends for all His brethren, as when the Lord wished to save His people by means of Moses and Aaron.

Further, He wishes to unite in the closest way the friends of Christ to the mystery of His redemption. Jesus does not live the mystery of His Agony, His Crucifixion, and His Burial by Himself alone, but He does so in union with His Mother, with John, and the holy women, indeed with all His disciples and all those who are freely and lovingly willing to be His disciples. This, too, is an act of mercy and superabundant love. For, from the standpoint of justice, the sacrifice of Christ fully and perfectly suffices. It is perfect and realizes perfect redemption. Mary was asked to become associated in it not in order to complete Christ's work of reparation and satisfaction, as though something was lacking in Him, but in order to carry out His overflowing mercy. To allow Mary to cooperate in her Son's work and live this mystery is to allow her to share a new intimacy and more perfect friendship with Him. Perfect friendship requires this friendly cooperation, since friends are associated together by doing the same work.

Then, the sacrifice of the Cross is the supreme work of God's mercy because this sacrifice, while a work of filial adoration, is also a means to free men from sin—the merciful gift of Christ to His brethren for those He has come to redeem. The mystery of the Eucharist expresses and fulfills this gift in the truest and most effective way. Christ wishes to give Himself to us under the form of bread and wine, as our food and drink. The Eucharist continues the Cross for us. The merciful gift of Christ, giving Himself to His members, is also the gift which the Father makes to us of His beloved Son. The Father makes this gift to those who have refused to obey Him, who have offended Him and crucified His Son, who have revolted against His Law and His will. He is not satisfied with forgiving their sins but wishes to make use of these pardoned sins in order to give them more love, to communicate divine life to them in full.

The liturgy does not hesitate to sing "O happy fault, which has given us such a Savior." That is how the mercy of Christ, the Good Shepherd of His sheep, and especially of the lost sheep, reveals to us the mercy of God, the Father of all mercy—He who is the principle Good Shepherd. The parable of the prodigal son shows us the mercy of the Father, which receives back the prodigal, forgives him, embraces him, clothes him with the wedding garment, and kills the fatted calf (Lk. 15:11-32). That is how the Father receives His prodigals, His younger sons, on the Cross. Sinners are clothed anew through the royal blood of Christ and are fed with His body and His heart. Were it possible, the good angels—the elder sons—who are always in the Father's house, would be jealous.

By the sacrifice of the Cross, we can, then, contemplate the mystery of God's fatherly mercy, unveiling God's overflowing goodness and love. To say that a person is merciful is not only to say that He is good, but that He is good in such a way as to comfort the misery of those around Him; it is to express a full, perfect, overflowing goodness. Mercy can only be used to describe one who is "superior" in the order of goodness. Hence, mercy is only perfectly true of God, for God is highest in the order of goodness, supreme and infinite in goodness.

By declaring that God is merciful, I bear witness that God's goodness is such that He can come to the aid of every misery. He is even able to get rid of the cause of all unhappiness, sin. Not only is God capable by His goodness of getting rid of all misery, but He will get rid of it when He wills it. On the Cross, God forgave all the sins of mankind. God is not only merciful, but He is Mercy and Forgiveness, as He is Love—that is, He is the source of all mercy and forgiveness, and all mercy and forgiveness come from Him. Therefore, the mystery of Christ crucified and the mystery of the Eucharist are the direct effects, the masterpieces, of this fatherly mercy.

* * *

It is primarily in the mystery of Christ crucified that harmony is perfectly established between God's mercy and justice. In the Old Testament, for the most part, we find either works of justice or works of mercy. This is particularly clear in the story of Moses: on the one hand, the Lord wishes to free His people and save them, and, on the other hand, the Lord punishes Pharaoh, employing His justice toward him. On the Cross, the justice of God is shown in full vigor toward Christ suffering and crucified, and, at the same time, the fullness of mercy is also shown to Christ. Hence, the Psalm tells us: "Steadfast love and faithfulness will meet; righteousness and peace will kiss each other. Faithfulness will spring up from the ground, and righteousness will look down from the sky" (Ps. 85:10-11).

This severely strict justice is, as it were, all wrapped in mercy; it is wholly dependent on mercy, which comes first. Christ, out of mercy, is willing to be the Lamb of God, clothed with all the consequences of our sins. Justice is wholly directed toward mercy; mercy is then last and ultimate. Everything culminates in mercy. We may say that justice, even when most strict, is at the service of mercy, allowing mercy to be what it is and to flourish in a marvelous degree. If Christ had not satisfied for the sins of men, the mercy of the Father could not have been exercised toward Him so abundantly. He would not be our Savior; He would not have given Himself up in this way for each of us.

This order between justice and mercy, manifested so plainly on the Cross, perhaps makes us understand better how the wisdom of God's governance is shown in regard to Christ the Head and His mystical body. God's wisdom is a wisdom of love and mercy, which makes use of justice and the Law in order to be more pure and complete.

Thus, we can contemplate the mystery of God's wisdom, mercy, and justice. In God, these qualities are not indeed distinct in the way they are in man, when they balance one another. In God, they are identical with His being: God is wisdom, justice, and mercy. Hence, each of these qualities exist in God only in a perfect way, without, however, limiting one another. God is not sheer justice, "justice in itself," but He is justice, mercy, and wisdom.

While, as regards the works of God, we can speak of a reconciliation in God's acts between mercy and justice; in God Himself there is not merely harmony between these qualities but formal identity. Justice as applied to the being of God, which is God, far from involving any contradiction to His mercy, is formally identified with His mercy. In this lies the mystery of the perfection of God's being, containing in an eminent way all the perfections that apply to the creature; not in the sense of a sum of these perfections or of a whole of which they are parts, but as possessing them in an eminent unity, in absolute simplicity. The perfection of God's being is such that in God justice and mercy are identified.

Thus, it is not surprising that all the works of God are justice and mercy, that all His works reflect His justice and mercy. Some reflect one of these qualities more clearly, others reflect the other more clearly.

For this reason, some of the works of God are called works of justice, others works of mercy, but all reflect Him who is justice and mercy in wisdom.

THE SACRIFICE OF THE CROSS:
THE REVELATION OF THE FATHER'S OMNIPOTENCE AND HIS PRESENCE IN ALL THAT EXISTS

> But this is the attribute of God, the Highest and Almighty, and the living God, not only to be everywhere present, but also to see all things and to hear all, and by no means to be confined in a place; for if He were, then the place containing Him would be greater than He; for that which contains is greater than that which is contained. For God is not contained, but is Himself the place of all (Theophilus of Antioch, *To Autolycus,* II, III).[22]

> We acknowledge one God, uncreated, eternal, invisible, impassible, incomprehensible, illimitable, who is apprehended by the understanding only and the reason, who is encompassed by light, and beauty, and spirit, and power ineffable, by whom the universe has been created (Athenagoras, *Apology* [A Plea for the Christians], X, 1).[23]

---

22. In *The Anti-Nicean Fathers,* Vol. II (Edinburgh: T&T Clark, 2001), p. 95.

23. Ibid., p. 133.

An act of adoration puts man in the presence of His Creator, whose first quality is omnipotence. To create, in the strict sense, requires infinite power, at least if the act of creation consists in giving being without the collaboration of any pre-existing reality, i.e., from nothing. To create is—starting from nothing—to produce a being.

Every action presupposes a certain active power in him who exercises this action. The quality proper to this action manifests the quality proper to the power that it presupposes. Now, the quality proper to this primary action, an action on which all others depend, is unique. This action is an action which has need of neither support nor matter in order to exist, but which communicates being to its proper effect. This act of creation, therefore, presupposes a unique power, a power wholly active. The omnipotence of God expresses such entirely unlimited power, since it is directly ordered to being. It reaches—it can reach—all that exists, all that can exist. Hence, the quality proper to the Creator is to be One who acts upon being, One who is almighty.

This is in fact how God introduces Himself to Abraham, when He says: "I am El Shaddai, God Almighty; walk before me and be blameless."[24] The name El Shaddai seems to be the most primitive name given to God. This seems to confirm the traditional meaning of "God almighty."[25]

---

24. Gen. 17:1. Also Ex. 6:2-3: "I am the Lord. I appeared to Abraham, to Isaac, and to Jacob, as God Almighty, but by my name the Lord I did not make myself known to them."

25. "I am El Shaddai" is rendered by the Vulgate as *Ego Deus omnipotens.*

The first and fundamental revelation made to us in Scripture about God's mystery has to do with His creative activity. He is God, Creator of Heaven and earth.[26] We are shown the splendor of His work, how great and harmonious it is, in order that we may be able to know from this the power and grandeur of Him who made it. To man, created in His image and likeness, God has given power to rule over the fishes and birds. By this "power," man is like the Creator; by worship and the offering of first-fruits of the earth and of his flocks (two kinds of fruitfulness), man acknowledges that he is wholly dependent on the Creator, that his work can do nothing at all except through the help of God's omnipotence. It is entirely to be expected that the sacrifice of adoration, that first and fundamental act of man's religious life, should have to do with what is fundamental and first in the revelation of God's mystery: His omnipotence as Creator.

Each of the great sacrifices, described in the Old Testament and mentioned here, directly reveals an aspect of the mystery of God's omnipotence. The sacrifice of Abel reveals to us above all the power of Him who is the source of all fruitfulness, Lord of life and death. The sacrifice of Noah shows us the omnipotence of Him who is the Master of the human race and its destiny, Master of the world, and who can make use of the elements in the universe whenever He wishes. The sacrifice of Abraham reveals to us the omnipotence of Him who is greater than His gifts, however wonderful they

---

26. Gen. 1:1: "In the beginning God created the heavens and the earth." Heaven and earth are God's works. They come from Him; God is before them.

may be, of Him who is dependent on none of these gifts: He can demand that they be offered up, if He chooses and judges it right. The sacrifice of the Passover reveals to us the omnipotence of Him who, in some sense, is able to create anew the people of Israel, to give them their freedom and their true calling, in spite of the power of Pharaoh—in comparison with the omnipotence of God, the power of Pharaoh is nothing. The sacrifice of Elijah manifests overtly the omnipotence of the true God, omnipotence put at the service of prayer and adoration and showing their efficacy. It is an omnipotence of fire and love, that is, an omnipotence that listens to the prayer of those who call upon it and grants their request. The sacrifice of the seven brothers and of their mother manifests the omnipotence of Him who is able to give back life, to raise the dead.

While all true sacrifice makes man nothing in the presence of the mystery of his Creator's omnipotence, thereby giving him an intimate realization of God's omnipotence, the songs of praise and the canticles found in Scripture declare God's omnipotence and, further, give us striking accounts of this mystery.

Some passages, therefore, may be quoted here. In the Canticle of Moses, after the departure from Egypt, the omnipotence of the Lord is acknowledged and praised:

> Pharaoh's chariots and his host he cast into the sea; and his picked officers are sunk in the Red Sea. The floods cover them; they went down into the depths like a stone. Thy right hand, O Lord, glorious in power, thy right hand, O Lord,

shatters the enemy. In the greatness of thy
majesty thou overthrowest thy adversaries; thou
sendest forth thy fury, it consumes them like
stubble. At the blast of thy nostrils the waters
piled up, the floods stood up in a heap; the
deeps congealed in the heart of the sea. . . .
Thou didst blow with thy wind, the sea covered them; they sank as lead in the mighty
waters. "Who is like thee, O Lord, among the
gods? Who is like thee, majestic in holiness,
terrible in glorious deeds, doing wonders?
Thou didst stretch out thy right hand, the
earth swallowed them. . . . Terror and dread fall
upon them; because of the greatness of thy arm,
they are as still as a stone, till thy people, O
Lord, pass by, till the people pass by whom
thou hast purchased (Ex. 15:4-8, 10-12, 16).

As fire is the symbol of love and anger, so the arm of the
Lord (or His hand) symbolizes His power. (Ex. 32:11: Moses,
addressing the Lord, asks Him to remember His people,
whom "thou hast brought forth out of the land of Egypt with
great power and with a mighty hand.")

In the Canticle of Moses, just before his death, the Lord's
power does not cease to be declared, as, too, in that first
"Magnificat" of Hannah's canticle. The power of the Lord is
praised in the Psalms and by the prophets. This absolute
omnipotence, which nothing can resist, which can give life
and can give death, is always considered as belonging to the
true God, to the Lord alone. Idols, false gods, have no power.

I kill and I make alive; I wound and I heal; and there is none that can deliver out of my hand (Deut. 32:39). The Lord kills and brings to life; he brings down to Sheol and raises up (1 Sam. 2:6). The adversaries of the Lord shall be broken to pieces; against them he will thunder in heaven (1 Sam. 2:10). The Lord is my rock, and my fortress, and my deliverer, my God, my rock, in whom I take refuge, my shield and the horn of my salvation, my stronghold and my refuge, my savior; thou savest me from violence. I call upon the Lord, who is worthy to be praised, and I am saved from my enemies (2 Sam. 22:2-4).

The wrath of the Lord shakes the very foundations of the universe:

He bowed the heavens, and came down; thick darkness was under his feet. He rode on a cherub, and flew; he was seen upon the wings of the wind. He made darkness around him his canopy, thick clouds, a gathering of water. Out of the brightness before him coals of fire flamed forth. The Lord thundered from heaven, and the Most High uttered his voice. And he sent out arrows, and scattered them; lightning, and routed them. Then the channels of the sea were seen, the foundations of the world were laid bare, at the rebuke of the Lord, at the blast of the breath of his nostrils (2 Sam. 22:10-16).

Let the heavens praise thy wonders, O Lord, thy faithfulness in the assembly of the holy ones! . . . O Lord God of hosts, who is mighty as thou art, O Lord, with thy faithfulness round about thee? Thou dost rule the raging of the sea; when its waves rise, thou still-est them. Thou didst crush Rahab like a carcass, thou didst scatter thy enemies with thy mighty arm (Ps. 89:5, 8-10: Rahab is the name of a mythical monster personifying the sea [cf. Job 7:12]; it also signifies Egypt).

Thou turnest man back to dust, and sayest, "Turn back, O children of men! . . ." Thou dost sweep men away; they are like a dream, like grass which is renewed in the morning: in the morning it flourishes and is renewed; in the evening it fades and withers. For we are consumed by thy anger; by thy wrath we are overwhelmed. Thou hast set our iniquities before thee, our secret sins in the light of thy countenance (Ps. 90:3, 5-8).

The Lord reigns; he is robed in majesty; the Lord is robed, he is girded with strength. Yea, the world is established; it shall never be moved; thy throne is established from of old; thou art from everlasting (Ps. 93:1-2).

Yonder is the sea, great and wide, which teems with things innumerable, living things both small and great. There go the ships, and Leviathan which thou didst form to sport in it. These all look to thee, to give them their food in due season. When thou givest to them, they gather it up; when thou openest thy hand, they are filled with good things. When thou hidest thy face, they are dismayed; when thou takest away their breath, they die and return to their dust. When thou sendest forth thy Spirit, they are created; and thou renewest the face of the ground (Ps. 104:25-30).

I will now call to mind the works of the Lord, and will declare what I have seen. By the words of the Lord his works are done (Sir. 42:15).

If the great deeds of God in the past enable us to contemplate His power, the future, which must come, enables us to do so still better. The prophets, who announce the coming of the Lord, praise the splendor of His majesty. The omnipotence of the Lord will then appear with a splendor hitherto unknown. Then we shall understand that He alone is worthy to be exalted above all (see Is. 2:6-22). But before this coming, the terrible wrath of the Lord will come. This wrath, in its own way, shows God's power by revealing His supreme authority. All authority requires a certain power, and supreme authority requires absolute power.[27]

---

27. It would be interesting to analyze the different moments of the wrath of the Lord recorded by Scripture. These occasions reveal different aspects of the authority of God, who has been offended by the sins of men. They give us a better understanding of certain aspects of God's omnipotence.

> Behold, the Lord will lay waste the earth and
> make it desolate, and he will twist its surface
> and scatter its inhabitants (Is. 24:1).

> For the windows of heaven are opened, and
> the foundations of the earth tremble. The
> earth is utterly broken, the earth is rent asun-
> der, the earth is violently shaken. The earth
> staggers like a drunken man, it sways like a
> hut; its transgression lies heavy upon it, and it
> falls, and will not rise again (Is. 24:18-20).

The sacrifice of Christ and His Resurrection reveal to us
in a totally new way, and yet in continuity with the Old Testament revelation, the mystery of God's omnipotence. As a
sacrifice of love, containing in a more eminent way the perfections of all the sacrifices of the Old Testament, the sacrifice of the Cross shows us, as the other sacrifices did, every
aspect of the mystery of God's omnipotence. Through His
act of adoration, Jesus acknowledges that everything that
exists comes from God and depends on Him, that nothing
can occur without His almighty will. Jesus entirely surrenders
His human will to the will of the Father. He offers to the
Father His own human will in order to glorify the will of the
Father.

By the complete surrender of His own will, Jesus pays
homage to the supreme majesty of the Father. The *dominum*
over His human nature—made in the image of God—is
allowed to give way before the *dominum* of God, before God's
omnipotence. Thus, He declares the supreme rights of His
God over Himself, over the whole human race, over the

whole universe, of which He is King. Through Him, the whole human race, the whole universe, honors in its Head the almighty majesty of God. We see, then, how the eminent dignity of this sacrifice manifests, more than any of the others, the omnipotence of God's grandeur. The greater the value and price of the victim offered to God, the more the rights of God and His omnipotence are glorified by its immolation. The Lamb of God, offered up at the Agony and on the Cross, possesses unique and incomparable value; He is the true Isaac, the well-beloved son, not only of the patriarch Abraham, but of the whole human race, the true Isaac of mankind. He is that unique son, who is offered on the mountain to make us understand the absolute claim of God's will, the omnipotence of His will, which has rights over life and death. This Son of the promise given to Mary and to men is taken back by the Father when He wills. Men would have liked to make a human use of the divine gift of the Son, to enhance their own temporal glory. The Father takes Him back to make us understand the divine way in which we should use His gift of Love, to make us understand the omnipotence of His love, which need give account to no one, but which remains faithful amid the infidelities of men.

The Father takes back Him whom men have rejected in order to give Him in a still more wonderful way. His omnipotence is truly an omnipotence of love, unwearying, unchangeable, and faithful.

When, at the Praetorium, Pilate is astonished by the silence of Jesus and asks Him: " 'Do you not know that I have power to release you, and power to crucify you?' Jesus answered him, 'You would have no power over me unless it had been given you from above' " (Jn. 19:10-11). And He died, expressing His absolute trust in the loving omnipotence of the Father: "Father, into thy hands I commit my spirit!" (Lk. 23:46).

His adoration, being a filial adoration of love, reveals to us in a new way the omnipotence of the Father's love. Of course, the same mystery of the Creator's omnipotence is declared and manifested, as certain outward facts make clear: "There was darkness over the whole land until the ninth hour" (Lk. 23:44); and: "And behold, the curtain of the Temple was torn in two, from top to bottom; and the earth shook, and the rocks were split; the tombs also were opened" (Mt. 27:51-52).

This sacrifice truly bears witness, as did that of Elijah on Mount Carmel, that the Lord is the only true God and that He who had just committed His soul into the hands of the Father was the holy one of God, His messenger, whom men did not receive. The centurion gave glory to God: " 'Certainly this man was innocent!' And all the multitudes who assembled to see the sight, when they saw what had taken place, returned home beating their breasts" (Lk. 23:47-48).

Above all, however, in this sacrifice is manifested the power of the Father's love; God's fatherly omnipotence, the omnipotence of His loving heart, is revealed. Thus, a much more inward and profound aspect of the mystery of God's omnipotence is reached and communicated to us. In order to get a clear grasp of these two aspects of the mystery, we would have to compare the theophanies of the Old Testament and that of Christmas. In the Old Testament, the theophanies were usually accompanied by noisy, visible manifestations that witness to the omnipotence of the Creator-God. We have only to think of the great theophany of Mount Sinai. It is truly the omnipotence of the Creator, the majesty of the Lord, King of the universe, which is manifested.

In the New Testament, God first comes to dwell among us without any external manifestation. Only the fiat of Mary, which remains a secret, is demanded. The virgin motherhood of Mary, miraculous indeed but concealed by the presence of Joseph, is the means employed by God's wisdom for His new presence among men. God comes to dwell among us, to share our home, taking possession of our earth in the most quiet yet realistic way. He really takes root in Mary and, through her, in our human race. Yet all remains hidden, veiled, silent. . . . No one but Mary can know of it. It is not a passing theophany but a dwelling among us that is secret, intimate, and complete, a taking possession forever of human nature by God Himself. Human nature is assumed by God and becomes His secret hidden temple, *in sinu Mariae.*

At Christmas, the face of God appears in the features of a young child, looking at His mother, who loves Him. The almighty hand of God, His "arm," is seen in and through the delicate hand of a small child, the weak arm of a child.

This wonderful theophany, more extraordinary than that of Mount Sinai, takes place in the silence of the night, in a poor stable, a shelter for cattle, in solitude. The omnipotence of God, the Creator, is veiled under the appearance of a little child in order to show only the most intimate love. Nothing more is seen of God's omnipotence; it is wholly at the service of love, hiding under the features of weakness of a little child in order to let love have full scope. The song of the angels, the star of the Magi, the miraculous birth of Jesus tell us that the omnipotence of God is at work, that it is present and active, but that it acts in the shadow of love, fulfilling the demands of the silence, intimacy, and proximity of love.

It is not surprising that on the Cross we find this same law of God's governance: love absorbs all; omnipotence is present, and it acts in a divine way to allow love to take all. Here, again, the mystery of the Eucharist helps us understand the Cross. In this mystery, the omnipotence of the Creator is present and active. It performs the amazing miracle of transubstantiation (the substance of the bread is changed into the substance of Christ's body); but it is all for the sake of the gift of love, allowing love to be given to us as bread, nourishment which we use the most. On the Cross, omnipotence is at work to allow the Lamb to be a victim of love to the fullest extent, to allow the heart of Jesus to be the ultimate victim. The revelation of the loving omnipotence of the Father, King of hearts, King of the secrets of hearts, is indeed manifested to us here. The majesty of God is not only the majesty of the Creator, but above all, it is the majesty of the Father, of Him who is love. It is the majesty and triumph of love. The authority and omnipotence of God are not only those of the Creator, but they are above all those of the Father, of Him who is love. It is the authority and omnipotence of love. Hence, this majesty, this authority, and this omnipotence cannot be further manifested by outward, extraordinary signs; they can be manifested only through intimacy and poverty.

In the mystery of the Resurrection are present these two aspects of the mystery of God's omnipotence, which complete one another—the omnipotence of the Creator and that of the Father. The Resurrection is the work of a creative omnipotence which creates everything anew, and it is also the work of an omnipotence of love. All is created anew, to glorify and manifest love. The glorified body of the risen Jesus is the living monstrance of His love for the Father and for us. His body is the splendor of the Son's love for the Father and for us. It is a new creation in love, a direct source of love, filled with the light of love. The omnipotence of the Father is at work there; it is His masterpiece of beauty and of love.

Thus, we can understand better how omnipotence and love are but one in God. Omnipotence and love are identical. Nevertheless, when we say that God is almighty, we express something different from when we say that God is Love. To declare that God is almighty is to assert that He depends on no one and that everything depends on Him, that He can accomplish whatever He wills in His wisdom. For this reason, Scripture tells us that nothing is impossible for God. God can always "make happen" what He pleases, for His good pleasure is always in accord with His wisdom. Hence, His absolute power, which is the prerogative of the first cause, expresses above all the sovereign power of domination: everything depends radically on Him, and He can depend on no one, for He is first.

This almighty power, which characterizes the first cause, lets us grasp the absolute autonomy of God. Yet we must never separate in God the omnipotence which characterizes the first cause and the omnipotence of love. For in God His love is His being, and His being is His love. The sovereign dominion of God is a sovereign dominion of one who is love. God is almighty love, as He is almighty being. In every creature there is a real distinction between power and love, although ordinarily there should be no opposition between these two qualities but rather a due order. Power is directed toward love and presupposes it. It is, as it were, wrapped in love. Sin introduces at first a certain opposition between these qualities, between the realm of affectivity and the realm of efficiency, and inverts the order willed by God. The sinner puts love at the service of efficiency. Then man is no longer the image of God but the image of Lucifer, who no longer loves but rather seeks to "do," who now lives only in the desire to bring about a new world. He believes he is the prince of this world.

We might suppose that, on account of His sovereign majesty and omnipotence, God is far from creatures, far from the heart and intelligence of man. It is true that certain statements in Scripture might make us think that God, at certain moments, is far from His creatures, while at other moments He is near them.

Solomon, after building the Temple to be the house of God, asked the question:

> "But will God indeed dwell on the earth? Behold, heaven and the highest heaven cannot contain thee; how much less this house which I have built! Yet have regard to the prayer of thy servant and to his supplication, O Lord

my God, hearkening to the cry and to the prayer
which thy servant prays before thee this day"
(1 Kings 8:27-28).

In the Psalms, we often find an appeal expressing the fear
that God is far away, hidden from him who invokes Him:

"Hear my prayer, O Lord; let my cry come to
thee! Do not hide thy face from me in the day
of my distress! Incline thy ear to me; answer
me speedily in the day when I call" (Ps.
102:1-2). "Why dost thou stand afar off, O
Lord? Why dost thou hide thyself in times of
trouble?" (Ps. 10:1). "Wilt thou forget me for
ever? How long wilt thou hide thy face from
me?" (Ps. 13:1). "My God, my God, why hast
thou forsaken me?" (Ps. 22:1).

This fear which man experiences seems to be justified by
the very words of God. After Adam's sin, the Lord sought him
in the garden. Adam hid himself, and God called to him:
"Where are you?" as though God did not know where he was;
on account of His omnipotent majesty it sometimes appears
that God is remote from man.

Nevertheless, if we consider the mystery of His majesty
and omnipotence, that of God as Creator as well as that of
God the Father, we can easily understand that, through His
almighty power, God can be present in a unique and intimate
way to all that can exist and that He is in fact present to all
that exists. The mystery of adoration makes us draw life from
His presence. Scripture reveals to us this presence of God

in all His works in a clear and often very realistic way. Some specially significant passages may be quoted here.

God appeared to Jacob in a dream and told him:

> "Behold, I am with you and will keep you wherever you go, and will bring you back to this land; for I will not leave you until I have done that of which I have spoken to you." Then Jacob awoke from his sleep and said, "Surely the Lord is in this place; and I did not know it" (Gen. 28:15-16).

When God appeared to Moses, He claimed possession of the place where He appeared, and this ground was "holy" (Ex. 3:5). God said He had seen the misery of the people of Israel and that He would be with Moses in the mission He entrusted to him. He gave him a sign that Moses might know of His presence.

Mount Sinai, also, seemed a place where God dwelt: "Moses went up to God, and the Lord called to him out of the mountain" (Ex. 19:3). "And the Lord came down upon Mount Sinai, to the top of the mountain; and the Lord called Moses to the top of the mountain, and Moses went up" (Ex. 19:20).

The Lord told Moses to build Him a sanctuary, that He might dwell among His people: "And let them make me a sanctuary, that I may dwell in their midst" (Ex. 25:8). This sanctuary was to possess an ark, in which Moses should place the written Law. The Lord said: "There I will meet with you, and from above the mercy seat, from between the two cherubim that are upon the ark of the testimony, I will speak with you of all that I will give you in commandment for the people of Israel" (Ex. 25:22). We can understand the words of the psalmist: "O Lord, who shall sojourn in thy tent? Who shall dwell on thy holy hill?" (Ps. 15:1).

When Israel was settled in the promised land, Solomon changed the sanctuary of the Lord into the Temple, that it might be His house, His holy dwelling-place: "I have built thee an exalted house, a place for thee to dwell in for ever" (1 Kings 8:13).

Solomon, while asking the Lord in prayer to fulfill His promise and dwell in the Temple built for the glory of His name, acknowledged that the heavens could not contain God. The Psalm of David, praising the bounty of the Creator, is plain: "O Lord, our Lord, how majestic is thy name in all the earth! Thou whose glory above the heavens is chanted by the mouth of babes and infants" (Ps. 8:1-2).

The Lord answered the prayer of Solomon: "I have consecrated this house which you have built, and put my name there forever; my eyes and my heart will be there for all time. . . . But if you turn aside from following me, you or your children, and do not keep my commandments and my statutes which I have set before you . . . the house which I have consecrated for my name I will cast out of my sight; and Israel will become a proverb and a byword among all peoples" (1 Kings 9:3, 6-7).

The fact that the Temple was the principal liturgical sanctuary where God dwelt did not prevent God from continuing to appear to whomever He willed and wherever He willed. This is plain in the lives of the prophets, and an example is God's meeting with Elijah. Elijah fled in fear to the desert to save his life, and then he begged the Lord to come and take him. The Lord commanded him to go to Mount Horeb:

> "Go forth, and stand upon the mount before the Lord." And behold, the Lord passed by, and a great and strong wind rent the mountains, and broke in pieces the rocks before the Lord, but the Lord was not in the wind; and after the wind an earthquake, but the Lord was not in the earthquake; and after the earthquake, a fire, but the Lord was not in the fire; and after the fire a still small voice. And when Elijah heard it, he wrapped his face in his mantle and went out and stood at the entrance of the cave. And behold, there came a voice to him (1 Kings 19:11-13).

The Lord seems to come and dwell in certain places successively, without however being limited and stuck to these places. These places were at first natural "high places," and later on they were places built by the people of God. But in the Psalms, God Himself is regarded as a place of refuge for the poor and the wretched. He is a place of stability and strength for those in the battle: "The Lord is a stronghold for the oppressed, a stronghold in times of trouble" (Ps. 9:9); "thou hast founded a bulwark because of thy foes, to still the enemy and the avenger" (Ps. 8:2).

The true sanctuary of the Lord is the Lord Himself, who is above all we can conceive. The heaven of heavens is the true holy of holies. There are many passages in the Psalms which express this clearly:

He looked down from his holy height, from heaven the Lord looked at the earth, to hear the groans of the prisoners, to set free those who were doomed to die (102:19-20). Of old thou didst lay the foundation of the earth, and the heavens are the work of thy hands. They will perish, but thou dost endure; they will all wear out like a garment. Thou changest them like a raiment, and they pass away; but thou art the same, and thy years have no end (102:25-27). The Lord is high above all nations, and his glory above the heavens! Who is like the Lord our God, who is seated on high, who looks far down upon the heavens and the earth? (113:4-6).

Yet, we must not suppose that God is far away because He stoops to regard Heaven and earth and is "above the heavens." God sees all, hears all, and lives in close contact with all that exists:

He who planted the ear, does he not hear? He who formed the eye, does he not see? (94:9). The Lord knows the thoughts of man, that they are but a breath (94:11). O Lord, thou hast searched me and known me! Thou knowest when I sit down and when I rise up; thou discernest my thoughts from afar. Thou searchest out my path and my lying down, and art acquainted with all my ways. Even before a word is on my tongue, lo, O Lord, thou knowest it altogether. Thou dost beset me behind and before, and layest thy hand upon me (139:1-5). Whither shall I go from thy Spirit? Or wither shall I flee from thy presence? If I ascend to heaven, thou art there! If I make my bed in Sheol, thou art there! If I take the wings of the morning and dwell in the uttermost parts of the sea, even there thy hand shall lead me, and thy right hand shall hold me. If I say, "Let only darkness cover me, and the light about me be night," even the darkness is not dark to thee, the night is bright as the day; for darkness is as light with thee (139:7-12). Thou knowest me right well; my frame was not hidden from thee, when I was being made in secret, intricately wrought in the depths of the earth. Thy eyes beheld my unformed substance; in thy book were written, every one of them, the days that were formed for me, when as yet there was none of them (139:14-16).

This almighty knowledge of the Lord, this effective unlimited presence, proclaimed so magnificently in the Psalms of David, is asserted afresh by the prophets Jeremiah (17:9-10), Isaiah (41:10-29; 49:16-26; 30:1-3), Amos (9:1-6), as well as in the book of Job (12-14), and the book of Wisdom (10 ff.).

Let us simply quote the following passages from Isaiah and Jeremiah:

> But now thus says the Lord, he who created you, O Jacob, he who formed you, O Israel: "Fear not, for I have redeemed you; I have called you by name, you are mine. When you pass through the waters I will be with you; and through the rivers, they shall not overwhelm you; when you walk through fire you shall not be burned, and the flame shall not consume you. For I am the Lord your God, the Holy One of Israel, your Savior" (Is. 43:1-3).

> "Am I a God at hand," says the Lord, "and not a God afar off? Can a man hide himself in secret places so that I cannot see him?" says the Lord. "Do I not fill heaven and earth?" (Jer. 23:23-24).

With the mystery of the Incarnate Word, the mystery of the presence of God in a place—in a sanctuary, in the Temple—culminates in a wonderful way. This new sanctuary was indeed Mary, in whom the mystery of the Incarnate Word was realized, this new presence of God among men. This presence was at first hidden within Mary, the presence of a child to his mother. It was a visible presence of the Child-God at Christmas, in poverty, since mankind refused to receive Him. Mary, Joseph, and the shepherds were alone to live this wonderful presence. God was then present to mankind as a child is present to his mother, as a child gives himself to his mother, in order to reveal to us how He is present to men, how He wishes to be Emmanuel, "God with us" (Mt. 1:23). The whole hidden life of Jesus is a life of presence to Mary and Joseph, presence of God in the simplicity of daily family life.

The active presence of Christ in His apostolic life to His disciples by means of His miracles and His preaching and teaching is, once again, a sign of the presence of the Father, who draws men and enlightens their minds and hearts in order to bring them to the Father's house. (Cf. Lk. 9:28-36; Mk. 9:2-8; Mt. 17:1-8. We should also understand the mystery of the Transfiguration in the apostolic life of Christ as a mystery of presence.)

Clearly, however, it is especially in the mystery of the Crucifixion and Resurrection that Christ reveals to us the mystery of the lasting, efficacious, and loving presence of the Father to each of us and to the whole world. On the Cross and in the Resurrection, He is indeed the sacrament of the Father's presence, as the mystery of the Eucharist makes fully explicit to us.

On the Cross, as the representative of the Father who has seen the misery of His people, and who wishes to de-liver them from the slavery of sin, He is the new Moses, who saves men by taking their place when condemned to death, forsaken by God, and rejected by men. He is present in a still more wonderful way than at Christmas. He is present as Savior, making reparation for our sins and giving us the love of the Father, associating us in His life: "Truly, I say to you, today you will be with me in Paradise" (Lk. 23:43). This presence is that of the Father of all mercy, who sees the misery of His people and makes use of their misery to come near them, to help them actively and effectively by means of His omnipotence. He gives them a new life. The Resurrection of Christ shows us how far the power of the Almighty reaches. The affective presence of love is real to the fullest extent.

This presence is only brought about for us to the extent that we wish to live in union with the heart of Christ, to the extent that we share in His loving adoration as Son and in His love as the Good Shepherd giving His life for His sheep. It is truly through worship, in union with Christ crucified, that we realize how much He has been given to us, how present He is, how present God is to us, through Him and in Him, as Father of all mercy, almighty in His mercy.

We thereby discover in an ultimate way the mystery of the presence of God to us and to the whole world. The intimate presence of the child Jesus at Bethlehem is an effective symbol, a sacrament of the intimate presence of the Father to Mary: the gaze of her child Jesus shows her the love with which the Father looks upon her and upon men—for this child, through Mary, is given to all souls of good will, to all men who seek God's love. In a similar way, the presence of the blood-stained Christ crucified on the Cross is an effective symbol, a sacrament of the power of love, of mercy, of the Father's forgiveness to all men without exception, but especially to Mary, John, and the holy women. For the Lamb of God has borne the sins of all men; the Lamb of God gives Himself as the food of love to all those who wish to live on His love. The omnipotence of God, at the service of love and mercy, accomplishes on the Cross a unique gift and a unique presence, that of the Father welcoming His prodigal son, embracing him, and forgiving his sins. The reality is still greater than the parable.

On the Cross, the presence of the Father to Jesus crucified, to His beloved Son, brings about and manifests the presence of the Father to all sinful men. In the presence of the
Father, the beloved Son is seen as the prodigal son, so that the
prodigal son may live as a beloved son.

The mystery of the Eucharist, a mystery of presence,
enables us to understand better this presence of the Father's
love. When the Lord gave to His people the manna, a sign of
the Eucharist, He said to Moses: "I have heard the murmur-
ings of the people of Israel; say to them, 'At twilight you shall
eat flesh, and in the morning you shall be filled with bread; then
you shall know that I am the Lord your God' " (Ex. 16:12).

This mystery is the sacrament of the presence of the
Father. It shows us how close and substantial is this presence.
God is intimately present as Creator to all that exists, with an
active and acting presence that gives to everything its proper
being and maintains it. The mystery of the Eucharist implies
the miracle of transubstantiation: the substance of bread is
changed into the substance of the body of Christ. This miracle is a sign of the efficacy of God's word, which reaches the
center of all that is and on which all that is wholly depends.
God alone reaches in this way all that exists. Hence, to God
the Creator, there is no such thing as distance; all is open to
His eyes. Creating by His word and by His fiat: " 'Let there
be light'; and there was light" (Gen. 1:3), God sees all that is
in His light—"darkness is not dark to thee" (Ps. 139:12).
This intimate and luminous contact of God with all that
exists is necessarily direct, with no possible intermediary, for
this would be contradictory to the creative act. It is an act in
which the creature cannot cooperate, for, in regard to this act,

the creature is "pure effect"; the creature is pure capacity. This presence of God as Creator is always the same, from the first creative act revealed at the beginning of Genesis to the last creative act of the last soul God will create. Such presence cannot increase but exists absolutely and lasts as long as God wills to maintain the creation. Every visible miracle of God is a sign of this presence and manifests it. But, to the believer, the miracle of transubstantiation and the miracle of the Resurrection of Christ's body are the plainest effects of the presence of the Creator in all that exists.[28]

The adoration of Christ-Eucharist in spirit and truth allows us to live from the presence of the almighty Creator. It makes us discover that God is our true home and our only refuge.

The Christian, however, cannot stay simply at the presence of the almighty Creator, however great and wonderful and luminous it may be. The presence of the Creator should lead him on to discover the presence of the beloved Father's love and mercy, in which he can wholly abandon himself in loving worship.

In addition, the mystery of the Eucharist is intended to give us a practical lesson. The miracle of the transubstantiation of the bread into the body of Jesus is directed toward the mystery of the Eucharist, the gift of Christ's body as divine food. The Eucharist makes present to us the body of Christ,

---

28. We must always distinguish carefully between the presence of God as Creator in all that exists, and the presence of God in the souls of the just by grace, which is the special presence of God to His people, to His beloved Son, and to those whom Jesus has redeemed on the Cross and feeds with His body

of the Lamb of God who suffered on the Cross, of the Lamb glorified in Heaven, by giving this body to us as food. Plainly this presence and this gift are only for the "sons of God," the disciples of Christ, for those who believe in His word and in His merciful love. For him who believes in the word of Christ, the Eucharist is thus a presence of God through the gift of merciful love. God wills to feed His children Himself; this is "manna." And He feeds them by giving Himself as food, for a "son of God" can only be filled by God, by His Father. The Eucharist is the most excellent sign of the fatherly presence of God's merciful love for each particular person. God is concerned for each person with a fatherly care. He knows everyone as the Good Shepherd knows His sheep; He knows their sufferings, their difficulties, and their struggles; He knows what is good in each one. He knows them as a friend knows his friend, with a knowledge that is practical, affective, and loving. He knows them in order to help them and support them. Nothing escapes His knowledge: God sees all. God can make use of everything in order to help them. His omnipotence gives complete efficacy to His fatherly care.

In order to show how personally adapted and full of tenderness God's solicitude for each person is, a sign of this solicitude is given in the "manna," food par excellence, which "changed to suit every one's liking" (Wis. 16:21).[29] One can

---

29. Wis. 16:20-21: "Instead of these things thou didst give thy people the food of angels, and without their toil thou didst supply them from heaven with bread ready to eat, providing every pleasure and suited to every taste. For thy sustenance manifested thy sweetness toward thy children; and the bread, ministering to the desire of the one who took it, was changed to suit every one's liking."

be fully present to a friend only when he has this tender concern for him. Such solicitude enables us to act with a very interior gentleness. The fatherly tenderness of God really acts deep within, without any violence. Hence the gift of the manna is the sign of a loving presence full of solicitude.

This gift of "bread" also expresses how the presence of love requires and effects union of life between God the Father and the Son. The bread becomes the body of the one who feeds on it. When it is assimilated, it becomes identical with the one who makes use of it. The Eucharist, which gives us the body of Christ as food, shows us how Christ wishes to unite us to Himself, to make us live by His life. Unity of life should be brought about: "He who eats my flesh and drinks my blood abides in me, and I in him. As the living Father sent me, and I live because of the Father, so he who eats me will live because of me" (Jn. 6:56-57).

This presence of love can only be compared to the presence of the Father in relation to that of His only Son. The presence of the Father to His Son is the presence of friend to friend in its deepest and most intimate element. Loving worship in spirit and truth in union with the worship of the Cross, in and through the mystery of the Eucharist, allows us, through faith, to draw life from this presence of love and from the infinitely tender care of the Father. Worship is then carried out in a filial abandonment, through which we discover how much the merciful love of the Father surrounds us, supports us, feeds us, and transfigures us. By sin, man can place an obstacle in the way of this presence of the Father's love for His children. Hence, Scripture speaks of being estranged from God, of God's seeming to be absent and no longer seeming to know where man is. These are metaphorical ways of speaking to express the fact that man strays from God and does not wish to turn lovingly toward Him. In reality, it is not God who departs from man, but it is man who of his own accord closes the gates of his soul and his heart to the fatherly influence of God and His merciful love.

The presence of God as Creator obviously still remains even after sin—for, even though sin kills love, it does not make the sinner cease to exist. He continues as an existing being, a wanderer, it is true, who has missed the path to His Father's house, but one who continues all the same to exist and who lives in absolute dependence on his Creator. God as Creator cannot be driven away from His creature, for the creature cannot annihilate itself, since its existence is not its own but belongs to God alone. But God as Father, Merciful Love, Savior of men, can be driven from the heart of man by man himself, by his pride, which does not want to accept this merciful love. Man cannot kill the traces of God-Creator that are in him, but he can kill in his heart the loving and merciful fatherhood of his God.

THE SACRIFICE OF THE CROSS:
THE REVELATION OF THE ETERNITY AND HOLINESS OF THE FATHER

O God, our Lord, what is your name? He tells us: my name is "He who is." What must I understand by "He who is"? That I live eternally, and cannot change. For things change do not truly exist, because they do not remain what they are. That which is remains.

That which changes has been one thing, and will be another, but does not truly exist, because it is changeable. Thus, it is the divine immutability which has designed to reveal itself in the words "I am He who is" (St. Augustine, Sermon 6, 3, 4).

The years of God are not truly other than God Himself; the years of God are the eternity of God; eternity is the very substance of God, in which nothing can be subject to change. In it nothing has passed in such a way as no longer to be; nothing is to come, as not yet being. In God, a single word, is; not, has been or will be; for that which has been no longer is, that which will be is not yet; and all that is in God, is, and cannot but be (St. Augustine, *Super Psalmos* 101:11, 10).

To worship God is first and foremost to acknowledge the rights of the Creator over all that is. Worship in spirit and truth implies that man offers to God what is dearest to him. This includes not only the first-fruits of his labor but the labor and toil itself, in order to manifest to himself and before the whole human community that he acknowledges that the whole value of his work comes from God and that he can only cooperate in God's act. In this way, man's labor can become a great liturgy of adoration and praise to the glory of God as Creator.

Work—this cooperation of man with the world in order to transform it—gives an intense awareness of time and of the temporal nature of work, as well as of our dependence on time and the relative power of control we have over time (for we can organize it as seems good to us). Therefore, to offer our work to God implies the offering of our time. And this offering of time places us in the presence of the mystery of God's eternity. We can, for God's sake, burn the little time we have for living on earth, because God is eternal.

This mystery of God's eternity is one of the great qualities of God that we ought to contemplate the most, given the conditions of our present era—an era in which we claim to be able to discover the historical meaning of man's wayward ideas and theories, an era in which we have such a clear awareness of the temporal character of our human condition. Perhaps we are often in danger of assigning a too-absolute value to these problems, which are undoubtedly very human and very important but which gradually turn us away from the true absolute in the order of duration: eternity. For this reason, it is very necessary for the believer to return often to the mystery of God's eternity and, in the light of eternity, to gain a proper appreciation of human duration and its temporal character. Scripture constantly speaks of God as the God of eternity (Gen. 1:1), that is, as the God who will never pass away, as He who is the most ancient (we cannot think of a being older than God), as He who continues forever.

Eternity implies duration without end. A being with a beginning and an end cannot be eternal. A being with a beginning but continuing forever is immortal but not eternal. An eternal being is a being without any limitation to its duration. This, however, is only a negative definition of eternity. To be more accurate, we must say that an eternal being has

duration without end and without succession, that is, a full
and entire duration, all in a single instant. Therefore, we can
imagine eternity as an instant that lasts forever, a substantial
instant that never passes away, but is.

What we must bear in mind is that eternity is duration
of unique intensity, such that it can involve no succession.
When we have joy of extraordinary intensity, we can have
some notion of what is represented by intensity in duration.
That is only an image of eternity. When Scripture asserts that
the Lord is an eternal God, it obviously does not explain itself
in the above manner, but rather, it helps us have an idea of
eternity by contrasting its stability with succession in time.
Nevertheless, if we reflect on this repeated assertion, it is
clearly about the characteristic peculiar to the being of God,
whose duration is without limit and who possesses Himself
perfectly without succession. Genesis begins by saying: "In
the beginning, God created the heavens and the earth."
Hence God exists before the beginning of time in the universe—the earth and the heavens.

St. Augustine emphatically expresses this contrast:

> For, though Himself eternal, and without be-
> ginning, yet He caused time to have a begin-
> ning; and man, whom He had not previously
> made He made in time, not from a new and
> sudden resolution, but by His unchangeable
> and eternal design. Who can search out the
> unsearchable depth of this purpose, who can
> scrutinize the inscrutable wisdom, wherewith
> God, without change of will, created man,

who had never before been, and gave him an existence in time, and increased the human race from one individual? [. . .] For this is a depth indeed, that God always has been, and that man, whom He had never made before, He willed to make in time, and this without changing His design and will (St. Augustine, *The City of God,* 12, 14).[30]

In the story of Abraham, we are told that, at Beersheba, Abraham called on the Lord, the Eternal God (Gen. 21:33).

At the end of the Bible, in the book of Revelation, God introduces Himself as one who contains and judges all generations: " 'I am the Alpha and the Omega,' says the Lord God, 'who is and who was and who is to come, the Almighty' " (Rev. 1:8; cf. 4:8; 21:6; 22:13). God is also called He "who lives for ever and ever" (Rev. 4:9). The twenty-four elders worship Him.

The conflict between the Lord, the Eternal God, and the false gods—between Him who is before all creation and who lives forever and the idols, which last only for a time—is often declared by the prophets. In His canticle, Moses was the first to emphasize this. Speaking of the infidelities of Jacob, he says: "They sacrificed to demons which were no gods, to gods they had never known, to new gods that had come in of late, whom your fathers had never dreaded" (Deut. 32:17). Idols are nothing: "they can neither mar nor

---

30. In *Nicene and Post-Nicene Fathers,* First Series, Vol. 2 (Peabody, Massachusetts:

make thee." The Lord alone is "the true God; he is the living God and the everlasting King" (Jer. 10:10).

The psalmist and the prophets also contrast the Lord who lives forever with creatures who pass away and live only for a time: "My days are like an evening shadow; I wither away like grass. But thou, O Lord, art enthroned forever; thy name endures to all generations." (Ps. 102:11-12). "He has broken my strength in mid-course; he has shortened my days. 'O my God,' I say, 'take me not hence in the midst of my days, thou whose years endure throughout all generations!' Of old thou didst lay the foundation of the earth, and the heavens are the work of thy hands. They will perish, but thou dost endure; they will all wear out like a garment. Thou changest them like raiment, and they pass away; but thou art the same, and thy years have no end" (Ps. 102:23-27). "For a thousand years in thy sight are but as yesterday when it is past, or as a watch in the night. Thou dost sweep men away; they are like a dream, like grass which is renewed in the morning: in the morning it flourishes and is renewed; in the evening it fades and withers" (Ps. 90:4-6).

Speaking of the victories of the Lord, Isaiah writes: "Who has performed and done this, calling the generations from the beginning? I, the Lord, the first, and with the last; I am He" (Is. 41:4). "All flesh is grass, and all its beauty is like the flower of the field. The grass withers, the flower fades; when the breath of the Lord blows upon it. . . . The grass withers, the flower fades; but the word of our God will stand forever" (Is. 40:6-8).

"He who lives forever created the whole universe; the Lord alone will be declared righteous. To none has he given power to proclaim his works . . ." (Sir. 18:1-2, 4).

The stability of the universe can also act as a means to uplift us to the mystery of God's eternity: "The world is established; it shall never be moved; thy throne is established from of old; thou art from everlasting" (Ps. 93:1-2).

But beyond these comparisons and contrasts is proclaimed the mystery of the eternity of the Lord: "But the Lord sits enthroned forever, he has established his throne for judgment" (Ps. 9:7). "Lord, thou hast been our dwelling place in all generations. Before the mountains were brought forth, or ever thou hadst formed the earth and the world, from everlasting to everlasting thou art God" (Ps. 90:1-2). "Be mindful of thy mercy, O Lord, and of thy steadfast love, for they have been from of old" (Ps. 25:6). "Have you not known? Have you not heard? The Lord is the everlasting God, the Creator of the ends of the earth. He does not faint or grow weary, his understanding is unsearchable"(Is. 40:28). "Before me no god was formed, nor shall there be any after me. I, I am the Lord, and besides me there is no savior. . . . I am God, and also henceforth I am He; there is none who can deliver from my hand; I work and who can hinder it?" (Is. 43:10-11, 13). "For the Most High knows all that may be known, and he looks into the signs of the age. He declares what has been and what is to be, and he reveals the tracks of hidden things. No thought escapes him, and not one word is hidden from him. He has ordained the splendors of his wisdom, and he is from everlasting and to everlasting. Nothing can be added or taken away, and he needs no one to be his counselor" (Sir. 42:18-21). "Stand up and bless the Lord your God from everlasting to everlasting. Blessed be thy glorious name which is exalted above all blessing and praise" (Neh. 9:5).

In conclusion, we should mention the prayer of Jonathan in the second book of Maccabees, which expresses so well the eternity promised to the children of God:

> O Lord, Lord God, Creator of all things, who art awe-inspiring and strong and just and merciful, who alone art King and art kind, who alone art bountiful, who alone art just and al-mighty and eternal, who dost rescue Israel from every evil, who didst choose the fathers and consecrate them, accept this sacrifice. . . ." (2 Mac. 1:24-26).

The sacrifice of the seven brothers and their wonderful mother is itself an appeal to eternal life. This sacrifice and martyrdom is a living witness that declares the mystery of the eternal life of God in God Himself and in His elect. Before this mystery of eternal life, life in time is nothing.

The whole teaching of the New Testament consists in the promise of eternal life given to us by Christ Himself, who not only possessed in Himself, as the Word and the only Son of the Father, this eternal life, but who is life eternal.

St. John, in his prologue and throughout his Gospel, constantly reveals to us the mystery of the eternal life of the Word made flesh and the importance of this mystery for those who believe in Him.

The first witness to the Word made flesh by John the Baptist, the messenger of God, is full of meaning:

"This is he of whom I said, 'After me comes a man who ranks before me, for He was before me' " (Jn. 1:30). Christ's first teaching, given to Nicodemus, a Jewish notable and a

Pharisee, is plain: "And as Moses lifted up the serpent in the wilderness, so must the Son of man be lifted up, that whoever believes in him may have eternal life. For God so loved the world that he gave his only Son, that whoever believes in him should not perish but have eternal life" (Jn. 3:14-16).

The final teaching of John the Baptist repeats that of Jesus and is most emphatic: "He who believes in the Son has eternal life; he who does not obey the Son shall not see life" (Jn. 3:36).

The final teaching of Jesus given to His disciples before His Passion is a prayer to His Father: "Father, the hour has come; glorify thy Son that the Son may glorify thee; since thou hast given him power over all flesh, to give eternal life to all whom thou hast given him. And this is eternal life, that they know thee the only true God, and Jesus Christ whom thou hast sent" (Jn. 17:1-3).

The mystery of the Cross and Resurrection—that is, the lifting up of the Son of Man foretold to Nicodemus and the glorification of the Son prayed for to the Father—is indeed to the believer the great revelation of the mystery of eternity, of the eternal love of the Father, a revelation that is carried out by the gift of eternal life.

We should say still more exactly that the sacrificial martyrdom of the seven brothers and their mother is a living witness which shows that the will of the Father is eternal, that God Himself, in His mystery, is beyond all succession of generation and time. Therefore, this eternal will can demand the holocaust of our temporal life in order to give us eternal life sooner. God wisely demands the sacrifice of a lesser reality for one that is higher, the sacrifice of earthly life for eternal life;

but the opposite would be folly. Similarly, but in a more eminent way, the sacrificial martyrdom of Christ is a living witness which shows that the loving will of the Father is eternal,
that God Himself, in His mystery of love, is beyond all
change or alteration. The fact that Christ freely committed
His soul into the hands of His Father proves that He recognized that His temporal life, however splendid, was nothing
in comparison to the eternal life of the Father. This was the
life He longed for: "Father, glorify thou me in thy own presence with the glory which I had with thee before the world
was made" (Jn. 17:5).

Christ's martyrdom is thus the proof for us of the eternal life of the Father. Worshiping the Father, offering to the
Father His own life as a holocaust of love, Christ bears witness that the life of the Father is more than any earthly life,
that the life of the Father is eternal life—able to make use of
Christ's death to communicate to His human nature, to His
dead body, a new overflowing life, more perfect and divine
than that which He had received from Mary.

The Resurrection of Christ's body manifests and
declares that this life received from the Father is an eternal
life: "For we know that Christ being raised from the dead will
never die again; death no longer has dominion over him."[31]
In the Apocalypse, the glorified Christ declares, "I died, and

---

31. Rom. 6:9; cf. Acts 13:34-35: "And as for the fact that he raised him
from the dead, no more to return to corruption, he spoke in this way,
'I will give you the holy and sure blessings of David.' Therefore he says
also in another psalm, 'Thou wilt not let thy Holy One see corruption.' "
Cf. 1 Jn. 1:10; Heb. 2:14 ff.; Ps. 16:10.

behold I am alive for evermore, and I have the keys of Death and Hades" (Rev. 1:18).

To assert that the life of the Father is eternal life is to assert that this life has no need of increase in order to exist perfectly, that it has no need of modification. It is a perfect life, which possesses in itself and in complete immanence all the perfection of life. Eternal life is a life that will not change, but not due to lack of energy or efficacy; it is a life that will not change, and cannot change, because it is so perfect that it has in itself all the fullness of life. God alone is eternal life because God alone subsists in His own being, His own life. Being eternal life, He is the source of all life. For this reason, He is able to make use of Christ's death, as of that of the seven brothers and their mother, to communicate to the body of Christ, as to the bodies of the seven brothers and their mother, when He wills, a new, overflowing life, a real participation in eternal life and, consequently, a life victorious over all death.

The martyrdom of Christ, being the martyrdom of the beloved Son—of Him who is faithful to the end—proves in a special way that the love of the Father is eternal love that knows no change, a love that remains always the same, a love that is faithful. God is eternal in His love: He is the supremely Faithful One.[32]

By declaring that God possesses eternal life, that His love is eternal, we declare at the same time that, in His very being, God is eternal, that He lives eternity. Hence, in our

---

32. Cf. Deut. 7:9: "Know therefore that the Lord your God is God, the faithful God who keeps covenant and steadfast love with those who love him and keep his commandments, to a thousand generations."

changing, corruptible world, the Cross of Jesus is truly the sacrament of God's eternity, the sign given "in the last days" to show that God's eternity alone remains. This sign is the way leading us to the mystery of God's eternity. By means of the Cross, we can live the eternal life of God. This eternal life is given to us; God's eternal love is given to us. By means of the Cross, a crack is opened in the succession of human generations and of time; and the mystery of God's eternity, the mystery of eternal life and eternal love, can be caught sight of. It is communicated to us by faith, if we so desire.

The sacrifice of the Cross, therefore, brings us into the presence of the eternal God. It enables us to share in His eternal life and love and understand how this mystery of eternity contains in an eminent way all the riches spread throughout time. In a unity of life and love and in perfect simplicity, the eternity of God contains all that occurs gradually through successive generations.

The sacrifice of the Cross also brings us into the presence of the holiness of God. We cannot worship God without discovering and acknowledging His holiness, and recognition of God's holiness calls for adoration.

It is interesting to call to mind how God has gradually revealed His holiness to us and how man has gradually come to acknowledge and worship it. We will mention just a few aspects of this revelation, in order to give a better understanding of how the sacrifice of the Cross puts us in the presence of the loving holiness of the Father and the holiness of the whole Trinity.

The first time that Scripture speaks of holiness is during the incident of the burning bush. Astonished at the sight of the bush on fire yet not consumed, Moses decided to approach "and see this great sight," to see why this bush was not consumed. God called to him from the midst of the bush: " 'Moses, Moses!' Then He said, 'Do not come near; put off your shoes from your feet, for the place on which you are standing is holy ground' " (Ex. 3:3-5).

The presence of the Lord in the bush made it "an awesome place," a "holy ground," that is, ground consecrated to God, upon which one could not walk thoughtlessly. The obligation to take off his shoes meant that he must purify himself in order to approach God, to approach the place where God was found, because God is holy.

Everything that is near God, everything that is consecrated to Him, is to be considered holy. The most secret and hidden place in the Temple is to be consecrated to God and called the "Holy of Holies." Not only certain places but also certain days are to be consecrated to Him; the Sabbath is to be the Lord's day and must be kept holy (Ex. 20:8-11); "You shall keep the sabbath, because it is holy for you; everyone who profanes it shall be put to death" (Ex. 31:14).

The ark is regarded as consecrated to the Lord. It is holy. Profane persons cannot touch it without dying (2 Sam. 6:6-7). All objects used in the great liturgy of the Temple are regarded as consecrated and holy. Speaking of the tabernacle, the ark, the table with its utensils, the lampstand, the altar of incense, the altar used for burnt-sacrifices, the Lord commanded Moses: "You shall consecrate them, that they may be most holy; whatever touches them will become holy" (Ex. 30:29). The oil used for anointing was to be considered holy: "And you shall say to the people of Israel, 'This shall be my holy anointing oil throughout your generations' " (Ex. 30:31). The offerings made to the Lord were also "holy things," set apart for God and for the priests, in a certain sense (Num. 18:9).

There are also holy persons who are consecrated to God: the whole people of Israel, and especially the priests who belong to God (Ex. 19:6). Since they are a people consecrated to God, Israel must not worship idols. They are the people of the Lord (Deut. 7:6). Speaking of the sons of Aaron, the Lord said, "They shall be holy to their God, and not profane the name of their God; for they offer the offerings by fire to the Lord, the bread of their God; therefore they shall be holy" (Lev. 21:6).

The Lord Himself explained why all that is connected to Him and all that is consecrated to Him is holy: it is because He Himself is holy. Speaking of priests, He commands: "He shall be holy to you; for I the Lord, who sanctify you, am holy" (Lev. 21:8).

Holiness is one of the great attributes of the Lord, perhaps the supreme attribute that He reveals to His people in the Old Testament, for it is the principal attribute that governs every action of religion: "I am the Lord your God; consecrate yourselves therefore. . . . I am the Lord who brought you up out of the land of Egypt, to be your God; you shall therefore be holy, for I am holy" (Lev. 11:44-45). "You shall be holy; for I the Lord your God am holy" (Lev. 19:2). "You shall be holy to me; for I the Lord am holy, and have separated you from the peoples, that you should be mine" (Lev. 20:26). "You shall not profane my holy name, but I will be hallowed among the people of Israel; I am the Lord who sanctify you" (Lev. 22:32).

On account of the holiness of God that is at the heart of the whole covenant of Mount Sinai, this challenge for holiness was soon to take on a legal aspect—as a legal holiness. Thus, the prophets did not cease to call to mind that holiness is principally an inward attitude of the heart and of the will, for the holiness of God is the holiness of a Person, not of a Law.

The prophet Isaiah does not cease to declare the holiness of God: "Ah, sinful nation, a people laden with iniquity, offspring of evildoers, sons who deal corruptly! They have forsaken the Lord, they have despised the Holy One of Israel, they are utterly estranged" (Is. 1:4). "But the Lord of hosts is exalted in justice, and the Holy God shows himself holy in righteousness" (Is. 5:16).

In his great vision of the Lord, the prophet sees Seraphim before the throne of the Lord, each with six wings, two to veil its face, two to cover its feet, two to fly, who were crying out: "Holy, holy, holy, is the Lord of hosts; the whole earth is full of his glory" (Is. 6:3). "The light of Israel will become a fire, and his Holy One a flame; and it will burn and devour His thorns and briers in one day. The glory of his forest and of his fruitful land the Lord will destroy, both soul and body, and it will be as when a sick man wastes away" (Is. 10:17-18).

For Hosea, the holiness of God holds Him back from acting according to His anger, but here it is the very holiness of God that explains the power of justice against the "haughty eyes" of the king of Assyria. But, in regard to his people, "the poor worm" reduced to nothing after the exile, the Holy One of Israel is full of mercy: "I will help you, says the Lord; your Redeemer is the Holy One of Israel" (Is. 41:14).

In revealing Himself as the "Holy" One, the Lord expresses His absolute transcendence. He is the One who is set apart from all that is created, who cannot be touched by that which is created. He cannot be profaned. He is pure in His whole being, His whole life, His whole love. There is nothing impure in Him. God cannot enter into composition with what He is not. He is set apart. Hence, all that is consecrated to Him is taken out of ordinary, profane use. All that is consecrated to Him must be pure.

The holiness of God does not only mean that God is set apart from all that is profane, but also that He is set apart from all sin. Hence, sin is utterly opposed to God's holiness.

When God declares, however, that He is holy—when the prophets, and especially the prophet Hosea, proclaim His holiness—more is asserted than this negative aspect of being set apart; what is also asserted is that, since the Lord is holy, He is able to forgive through love and to sanctify whom He wills—to consecrate them and keep them for Himself. Thus, the holiness of God implies an eminent and overwhelming jealousy, which is able to attract us and finalize us in an exclusive way.

It is this aspect of God's holiness which Christ specially reveals to us in a new way during His earthly life and above all in the mystery of the Cross.

As a result of the mystery of the hypostatic union, Christ has a human nature, wholly consecrated to God. He is the anointed of God, "holy" in His whole being and His whole human nature (Heb. 7:26); his human nature is truly a "holy ground." Hence, He can manifest to us in a special way the mystery of God's holiness, the mystery of the Father's holiness. Our Lord told His disciples to address the Father in this way: "Hallowed be thy name" (Mt. 6:9; Lk. 11:2-4).

In His great priestly prayer, Jesus calls on the holiness of the Father: "Holy Father, keep them in thy name, which thou hast given me, that they may be one, even as we are one" (Jn. 17:11). It is the holiness of the Father that draws those whom He loves with such jealousy as to unite them with Himself, in a union like that which exists between the heavenly Father and His beloved Son. And Jesus adds: "And for their sake I consecrate myself, that they also may be consecrated in truth" (Jn. 17:19).

In His sacrifice on the Cross, Jesus crucified, a holy victim, making amends for sin, glorifies the holiness of the Father and hallows His name—the fulfillment of what the Lord declared through His prophet: "And I will vindicate the holiness of my great name, which has been profaned among the nations, and which you have profaned among them; and the nations will know that I am the Lord, says the Lord God, when through you I vindicate my holiness before their eyes" (Ezek. 36:23).

Jesus reveals to us how the Father is set apart from all sin, how sin opposes His love. He reveals to us how the Father wishes to forgive and cleanse all who are sorry for their sins. The whole human race can be perfectly cleansed through the sacrificed Lamb. He reveals to us how the Father desires to consecrate, not only His own people, but all men, by a new covenant, a holy covenant in the blood and body of His Son. In the blood of His Son, the Father creates all men anew; He creates them anew in the image of His only beloved Son, with whom He is well pleased. He creates them anew by uniting them to His Son as living members of a single Body, sharing in the life of the Son, living by His Spirit of love. Thus the Father unites men to Himself in an utterly new way and fulfills the prayer of His Son: "Holy Father . . . that they may be one, even as we are one." Here is the fruit of His overflowing holiness, which draws everyone jealously to Himself. It is on the Cross, in and through His crucified Son, that He draws all men, that He draws them and consecrates them in love in a totally exclusive way.

The sacrifice of the Cross reveals to us the threefold holiness of God—the holiness of the Father, the Son, and the Spirit: "Holy, holy, holy, is the Lord God Almighty, who was, and is, and is to come" (Rev. 4:8); the holiness of being set apart, the holiness of purification and of light, the holiness of unity and consecration. By revealing to us the holiness of the Father, Jesus reveals to us His own holiness as beloved Son, with whom the Father is well pleased, and He gives to us His Spirit, the Holy Spirit.

The vocation of every Christian is, therefore, a vocation to holiness: "As he who called you is holy, be holy yourselves in all your conduct; since it is written, 'You shall be holy, for I am holy' " (1 Pet. 1:15-16).

CONCLUSION

INTEGRATING all the perfections of the Old Testament sacrifices and going beyond them, the sacrifice of the Cross is indeed, for the Christian, the "wisdom of God"—a wisdom that allows him to worship "in spirit and truth" the one God, his Creator and his Father. It is a wisdom that allows him to contemplate and glorify all the splendors of his God and Father. The whole revelation of the Old Testament concerning the mystery of God and His attributes is truly fulfilled on the Cross. The Cross puts us in the presence of the God who is thrice holy and one, eternal, al-mighty, all-seeing, present to everything that exists, just and merciful, infinitely good, and simple. What had been revealed only partially and in outline is at once clearly manifested. In the presence of the Cross, man cannot remain indifferent. The three attitudes described by St. Paul still remain true.

> For the word of the cross is folly to those who
> are perishing, but to us who are being saved
> it is the power of God. For it is written, "I

will destroy the wisdom of the wise, and the cleverness of the clever I will thwart." Where is the wise man? Where is the scribe? Where is the debator of this age? Has not God made foolish the wisdom of the world? For since, in the wisdom of God, the world did not know God through wisdom, it pleased God through the folly of what we preach to save those who believe. For Jews demand signs and Greeks seek wisdom, but we preach Christ crucified, a stumbling block to Jews and folly to Gentiles, but to those who are called, both Jews and Greeks, Christ the power of God and the wisdom of God (1 Cor. 1:18-24).

The Cross is folly to the Gentiles, scandal to the Jews, wisdom to the believer. We may have experienced these three attitudes deeply within our own selves, and can do so again. That is normal. For the "Gentile" is the philosopher who reasons. And is there not always a "little philosopher" in each of us who reasons and wishes to judge everything by what he has understood? He always finds that the mystery of the Cross is folly, an absurdity, and that He should consider this meaningless "fact" as little as possible. He should disregard it and try to explain the world as it presents itself to us; He should try to explain man by his personal experience of "man" in himself and in those around him. This kind of "philosopher" could accept God as the Creator, as the first being and all-powerful; he could agree to worship Him inwardly, declaring His dignity and rights as Creator. Often, however, he stops there. The acts of adoration performed by Abel and Noah, if accepted, are acknowledged as primitive symbols of this spiritual worship directed to the one Creator and God. But true worship, "in spirit and truth," the adoration of Christ crucified, he cannot accept; for he does not grasp the true demands of divine love—a love of friendship, a jealous and personal love. He does not enter into the mystery of faithfulness, which alone gives meaning to the sacrifice of the Cross. It is not foolish or absurd to acknowledge that God is Love and that, in His jealous love, God demands the inward sacrifice of our way of judging. He demands the sacrifice of obedience so that His love may be able to have free reign. In our day, philosophers who have such a high regard for freedom can still accept the spontaneous adoration of a spirit turning to Him who is the Creator of the world. But they are opposed to a worship which takes the humble form of obedience and which expresses a love that, in order to be faithful, is willing to lose its splendor: the worship of the Crucified One, of Him who is despised, rejected by men, of Him who obeys the Father.

The worship of the Cross always remains a folly to the "philosopher." We must not try to humanize the Cross so as to make it more acceptable to the philosopher, for that would be to get rid of the mystery. We must accept that the Cross is wisdom only to the believer, and we must recognize that it is—and always will be—a mystery for our reason. We cannot confine the mystery of God within the limits of our reason. If this mystery is presented to us in all its plenitude, is it surprising that our poor intelligence should be wholly surpassed?

We ourselves have perhaps also experienced, within our very selves, how much the mystery of the Cross is a scandal! To a sensitive, affectionate person who lives by his feelings, the adoration of Christ crucified is not merely unbearable, but a scandal, a stumbling block, which holds him back and causes him to fall. Does the mystery of the Cross not seem to be in opposition to the instinctive motions of our sensibilities and our dreams? Nothing seems less natural to us. Nothing seems so violent, so "anti-human." If we let our human heart speak in accordance with its feelings and inclinations, it will always avoid taking into consideration the demands involved in the sacrifice of the Cross. We may have a certain religious sentiment at the level of affective sensitivity, which draws us toward religious things and which makes us love an attitude of devotion and prayer. But a religious sense of this sort is scandalized by the mystery of the Cross. If it claims to love God, this is really for the sake of the sensitive, human joy that we experienced during some liturgical ceremony. A religious sense of this kind may, of course, assume very different forms, ranging from the romantic feelings of one who is moved by the smoke of the incense and the atmosphere of a particular place of worship to the refined, aesthetic feeling of someone well-cultivated in religious matters, who enjoys a beautiful ceremony or the splendor of Gregorian chant. Attitudes such as these may perhaps become a path to a truer and deeper religious spirit; but if the person just remains focused on himself, his religious practices will never attain to a true act of adoration, directed to God the Creator.

While the philosopher, as such, cannot go beyond an adoration that considers God as Creator, the person who gets stuck in his religious feelings cannot go beyond an "image" which he makes of God. It is not surprising that he is scandalized by the realism of the sacrifice of the Cross, which attains God in His mystery of inner, jealous love. Here again we must not reduce the true God to our imaginary images, dreams, and artistic ideas. We must accept the fact that we cannot directly reach the One God through our imagination and artistic appreciation.

We must recognize that only faith in Christ crucified allows us to reach God in His personal mystery, in His mystery of merciful, just love, in His mystery of almighty, eternal love; and only faith allows us to live this mystery of God's love, given and communicated to us through the filial adoration of Jesus.

Such faith does not destroy our reason and intelligence. Quite the opposite, it intensifies our spiritual love, allowing it to become more itself. By loving God with supernatural, divine love, together with Christ crucified, we have a true love of ourselves and of those around us. Such love can possess a unique quality of affection and even efficacy, for it intimately unites our hearts to the Source of all love.

Our artistic appreciation is itself cleansed and strengthened, for it finds itself ennobled from within by the living faith which unites it to Him who is the masterpiece of God, to Him who—in His mystery of the Cross and in His mystery of the Resurrection—is truly the Glory of the Father.

To the believer, the adoration of Christ crucified is indeed the "wisdom" of God. It alone brings to fulfillment the different acts of worship of the Old Testament. It alone gives us direct access to the Kingdom of God, to the contemplation of His mystery and His attributes.

ABOUT THE AUTHOR

FATHER MARIE-DOMINIQUE PHILIPPE

FATHER Marie-Dominique Philippe was born in 1912 at Cysoing in Northern France and studied theology and philosophy at the Dominican College of Le Saulchoir. He entered the Order of Preachers in 1930 and was ordained priest in 1936. He taught from 1945 to 1982 at the University of Fribourg in Switzerland. His published works include studies of Aristotle, St. Thomas Aquinas, and the theology of the Immaculate Conception, as well as numerous other philosophical and spiritual works. In 1975, he founded the Congregation of the Brothers of St. John, a religious order devoted to contemplation and apostolic life. Soon after, he also founded the Contemplative Sisters of St. John and the Apostolic Sisters of St. John. The religious family now includes over one thousand members and has priories in over thirty countries all over the world. Father Philippe died on August 26, 2006 in the Novitiate House in France where he had devoted so many years to prayer and teaching.